# First NLPL Workshop on Deep Learning for Natural Language Processing (DL4NLP 2019)



NEALT Proceedings Series Volume 38

Turku, Finland
30 September 2019

**Editors:**

**Joakim Nivre**
**Filip Ginter**
**Stephan Oepen**
**Jörg Tiedemann**

ISBN: 978-1-5108-9443-3

**Printed from e-media with permission by:**

Curran Associates, Inc.
57 Morehouse Lane
Red Hook, NY 12571

**Some format issues inherent in the e-media version may also appear in this print version.**



Printed by Curran Associates, Inc. (2019)

For permission requests, please contact the Association for Computational Linguistics at the address below.

Association for Computational Linguistics
209 N. Eighth Street
Stroudsburg, Pennsylvania 18360

Phone: 1-570-476-8006
Fax: 1-570-476-0860

acl@aclweb.org

**Additional copies of this publication are available from:**

Curran Associates, Inc.
57 Morehouse Lane
Red Hook, NY 12571 USA
Phone: 845-758-0400
Fax: 845-758-2633
Email: curran@proceedings.com
Web: www.proceedings.com

DL4NLP 2019

# Proceedings of the First NLPL Workshop on Deep Learning for Natural Language Processing

photo: © The City of Turku, Seilo Ristimäki

30 September, 2019
University of Turku
Turku, Finland

**Editors:**

Joakim Nivre
Filip Ginter
Stephan Oepen
Jörg Tiedemann

**Publisher:**

Linköping University Electronic Press in series *Linköping Electronic Conference Proceedings*, No. 163
ISSN: 1650-3686, eISSN: 1650-3740

NEALT in series *NEALT Proceedings Series*, No. 38

**Indexed in ACL Anthology.**

# Introduction

The Nordic Language Processing Laboratory (NLPL; http://nlpl.eu) is a collaboration of university research groups in Natural Language Processing (NLP) in Northern Europe. Our vision is to implement a virtual laboratory for large-scale NLP research by (a) creating new ways to enable data- and compute-intensive Natural Language Processing research by implementing a common software, data and service stack in multiple Nordic HPC centres, (b) by pooling competencies within the user community and among expert support teams, and (c) by enabling internationally competitive, data-intensive research and experimentation on a scale that would be difficult to sustain on commodity computing resources.

One of the clear strengths of NLPL is its community-building component, with the very successful winter school being the highlight of the year for many of us. As these proceedings demonstrate, the NLPL community-building effort now also includes the first edition of what will hopefully develop into a series of regular workshops organized under the NLPL umbrella.

The purpose of this first NLPL workshop was to bring together researchers with a special interest in the deep learning techniques, specifically inviting also papers on computational and practical aspects of these methods. We are happy to be able to present seven peer-reviewed papers on diverse deep learning topics, together with the invited talks of Barbara Plank and Jussi Karlgren.

On behalf of the organizers,

Joakim Nivre, Filip Ginter, Stephan Oepen, Jörg Tiedemann

September 2019

**Organisers:**

*Chair:* Joakim Nivre

Leon Derczynski, Filip Ginter, Bjørn Lindi, Stephan Oepen, Anders Søgaard, Jörg Tiedemann

**Program Committee:**

Željko Agić, Ali Basirat, Johannes Bjerva, Hande Celikkanat, Mathias Creutz, Leon Derczynski, Filip Ginter, Christian Hardmeier, Mareike Hartmann, Jenna Kanerva, Andrey Kutuzov, Juhani Luotolahti, Joakim Nivre, Stephan Oepen, Alessandro Raganato, Yves Scherrer, Natalie Schluter, Miikka Silfverberg, Sara Stymne, Umut Sulubacak, Aarne Talman, Gongbo Tang, Jörg Tiedemann, Raul Vazquez, Erik Velldal, Aleksi Vesanto, Miryam de Lhoneux, Lilja Øvrelid

**Invited Speakers:**

Barbara Plank, IT University of Copenhagen, Denmark
Jussi Karlgren, Gavagai and KTH Royal Institute of Technology, Sweden

# Invited Talks

### Deep Transfer Learning: Learning across Languages, Modalities and Tasks

*Barbara Plank, ITU (IT University of Copenhagen)*

Transferring knowledge to solve a related problem is an extraordinary human ability. Yet, how can we build Natural Language Processing technology which can transfer to new conditions, such as learning to process a new language or learning to answer new types of questions? In this talk, I will present some recent work to addresses this ubiquitous challenge using neural networks for transfer learning. In particular, I will focus on cross-lingual learning for syntactic processing and work at the interface of language and vision, e.g., multi-task and continual learning for visual question answering.

### High-Dimensional Semantic Spaces and the Squinting Linguist

*Jussi Karlgren, Gavagai and KTH Royal Institute of Technology*

High-dimensional distributed semantic spaces have proven useful and effective for aggregating and processing visual and lexical information for many tasks related to heterogenous data generated by human behaviour or relevant for human information processing. Models to process such high-dimensional spaces have proliferated in recent years with impressive results on quite various tasks.

In general, a representation used in research should hold to some basic qualities.

- It should have descriptive and explanatory power;
- be practical and convenient for further application;
- allow generalisations to be made and analogies to be inferred;
- be reasonably true to human performance, providing defaults to smooth over situations where data are lacking and constraints where the decision space is too broad,
- perform seamlessly and incrementally online in face of novel data, allowing new features and new analyses to be incorporated without recompiling previous understanding.

High-dimensional semantic spaces are usually not designed with (all of) these qualities in mind.

Human language has a large and varying number of features of various regularity, incorporating both lexical items and constructions. The field of linguistics provides a large body of research to understand such regularities. Yet the models used to process human language disregard those regularities, starting from the general principle that they should be discovered rather than given and that learning should be in the form an end-to-end classifier from raw data to relevant categories. This principle is intuitively appealing, in view of the specificity and avowed situation- and task-independence of linguistic rules, but the tools built end up being black boxes and do not guarantee explanatory generality of the results.

This talk will discuss how tasks where human language is the most important source of information might do well to incorporate information other than the most typical lexical features, in effect providing a better input layer to recent neurally inspired models. This talk demonstrates how high-dimensional semantic spaces can accommodate several types of feature concurrently, and that the convenient computing framework can be used for hypothesis-driven research. Such models can represent broad ranges of linguistic features in a common integral framework which is suitable as a bridge between symbolic and continuous representations, as an encoding scheme for symbolic information.

# Table of Contents

# Mark my Word:
# A Sequence-to-Sequence Approach to Definition Modeling

**Timothee Mickus**
Université de Lorraine
CNRS, ATILF
tmickus@atilf.fr

**Denis Paperno**
Utrecht University
d.paperno@uu.nl

**Mathieu Constant**
Université de Lorraine
CNRS, ATILF
mconstant@atilf.fr

## Abstract

Defining words in a textual context is a useful task both for practical purposes and for gaining insight into distributed word representations. Building on the distributional hypothesis, we argue here that the most natural formalization of definition modeling is to treat it as a sequence-to-sequence task, rather than a word-to-sequence task: given an input sequence with a highlighted word, generate a contextually appropriate definition for it. We implement this approach in a Transformer-based sequence-to-sequence model. Our proposal allows to train contextualization and definition generation in an end-to-end fashion, which is a conceptual improvement over earlier works. We achieve state-of-the-art results both in contextual and non-contextual definition modeling.

## 1 Introduction

The task of *definition modeling*, introduced by Noraset et al. (2017), consists in generating the dictionary definition of a specific word: for instance, given the word "*monotreme*" as input, the system would need to produce a definition such as "*any of an order (Monotremata) of egg-laying mammals comprising the platypuses and echidnas*".[1] Following the tradition set by lexicographers, we call the word being defined a *definiendum* (pl. *definienda*), whereas a word occurring in its definition is called a *definiens* (pl. *definientia*).

Definition modeling can prove useful in a variety of applications. Systems trained for the task may generate dictionaries for low resource languages, or extend the coverage of existing lexicographic resources where needed, e.g. of domain-specific vocabulary. Such systems may also be able to provide reading help by giving definitions for words in the text.

A major intended application of definition modeling is the explication and evaluation of distributed lexical representations, also known as word embeddings (Noraset et al., 2017). This evaluation procedure is based on the postulate that the meaning of a word, as is captured by its embedding, should be convertible into a human-readable dictionary definition. How well the meaning is captured must impact the ability of the model to reproduce the definition, and therefore embedding architectures can be compared according to their downstream performance on definition modeling. This intended usage motivates the requirement that definition modeling architectures take as input the embedding of the *definiendum* and not retrain it.

From a theoretical point of view, usage of word embeddings as representations of meaning (cf. Lenci, 2018; Boleda, 2019, for an overview) is motivated by the distributional hypothesis (Harris, 1954). This framework holds that meaning can be inferred from the linguistic context of the word, usually seen as co-occurrence data. The context of usage is even more crucial for characterizing meanings of ambiguous or polysemous words: a definition that does not take disambiguating context into account will be of limited use (Gadetsky et al., 2018).

We argue that definition modeling should preserve the link between the *definiendum* and its context of occurrence. The most natural approach to this task is to treat it as a *sequence-to-sequence* task, rather than a *word-to-sequence* task: given an input sequence with a highlighted word, generate a contextually appropriate definition for it (cf. sections 3 & 4). We implement this approach in a Transformer-based sequence-to-sequence model that achieves state-of-the-art performances (sections 5 & 6).

[1] Definition from Merriam-Webster.

## 2 Related Work

In their seminal work on definition modeling, Noraset et al. (2017) likened systems generating definitions to language models, which can naturally be used to generate arbitrary text. They built a sequential LSTM seeded with the embedding of the *definiendum*; its output at each time-step was mixed through a gating mechanism with a feature vector derived from the *definiendum*.

Gadetsky et al. (2018) stressed that a *definiendum* outside of its specific usage context is ambiguous between all of its possible definitions. They proposed to first compute the AdaGram vector (Bartunov et al., 2016) for the *definiendum*, to then disambiguate it using a gating mechanism learned over contextual information, and finally to run a language model over the sequence of *definientia* embeddings prepended with the disambiguated *definiendum* embedding.

In an attempt to produce a more interpretable model, Chang et al. (2018) map the *definiendum* to a sparse vector representation. Their architecture comprises four modules. The first encodes the context in a sentence embedding, the second converts the *definiendum* into a sparse vector, the third combines the context embedding and the sparse representation, passing them on to the last module which generates the definition.

Related to these works, Yang et al. (2019) specifically tackle definition modeling in the context of Chinese—whereas all previous works on definition modeling studied English. In a Transformer-based architecture, they incorporate "sememes" as part of the representation of the *definiendum* to generate definitions.

On a more abstract level, definition modeling is related to research on the analysis and evaluation of word embeddings (Levy and Goldberg, 2014a,b; Arora et al., 2018; Batchkarov et al., 2016; Swinger et al., 2018, e.g.). It also relates to other works associating definitions and embeddings, like the "reverse dictionary task" (Hill et al., 2016)—retrieving the *definiendum* knowing its definition, which can be argued to be the opposite of definition modeling—or works that derive embeddings from definitions (Wang et al., 2015; Tissier et al., 2017; Bosc and Vincent, 2018).

## 3 Definition modeling as a sequence-to-sequence task

Gadetsky et al. (2018) remarked that words are often ambiguous or polysemous, and thus generating a correct definition requires that we either use sense-level representations, or that we disambiguate the word embedding of the *definiendum*. The disambiguation that Gadetsky et al. (2018) proposed was based on a contextual cue—ie. a short text fragment. As Chang et al. (2018) notes, the cues in Gadetsky et al.'s (2018) dataset do not necessarily contain the *definiendum* or even an inflected variant thereof. For instance, one training example disambiguated the word "*fool*" using the cue "*enough horsing around—let's get back to work!*".

Though the remark that *definienda* must be disambiguated is pertinent, the more natural formulation of such a setup would be to disambiguate the *definiendum* using its actual context of occurrence. In that respect, the *definiendum* and the contextual cue would form a linguistically coherent sequence, and thus it would make sense to encode the context together with the *definiendum*, rather than to merely rectify the *definiendum* embedding using a contextual cue. Therefore, definition modeling is by its nature a sequence-to-sequence task: mapping contexts of occurrence of *definienda* to definitions.

This remark can be linked to the distributional hypothesis (Harris, 1954). The distributional hypothesis suggests that a word's meaning can be inferred from its context of usage; or, more succinctly, that "you shall know a word by the company it keeps" (Firth, 1957). When applied to definition modeling, the hypothesis can be rephrased as follows: the correct definition of a word can only be given when knowing in what linguistic context(s) it occurs. Though different kinds of linguistic contexts have been suggested throughout the literature, we remark here that sentential context may sometimes suffice to guess the meaning of a word that we don't know (Lazaridou et al., 2017). Quoting from the example above, the context "*enough _____ around—let's get back to work!*" sufficiently characterizes the meaning of the omitted verb to allow for an approximate definition for it even if the blank is not filled (Taylor, 1953; Devlin et al., 2018).

This reformulation can appear contrary to the original proposal by Noraset et al. (2017), which conceived definition modeling as a "word-to-sequence task". They argued for an approach related to, though distinct from sequence-to-sequence architectures. Concretely, a specific encoding procedure was applied to the *definiendum*, so that it could be used as a feature vector during generation. In the simplest case, vector encoding of the *definiendum* consists in looking up its vector in a vocabulary embedding matrix.

We argue that the whole context of a word's usage should be accessible to the generation algorithm rather than a single vector. To take a more specific case of verb definitions, we observe that context explicitly represents argument structure, which is obviously useful when defining the verb. There is no guarantee that a single embedding, even if it be contextualized, would preserve this wealth of information—that is to say, that you can cram all the information pertaining to the syntactic context into a single vector.

Despite some key differences, all of the previously proposed architectures we are aware of (Noraset et al., 2017; Gadetsky et al., 2018; Chang et al., 2018; Yang et al., 2019) followed a pattern similar to sequence-to-sequence models. They all implicitly or explicitly used distinct submodules to encode the *definiendum* and to generate the *definientia*. In the case of Noraset et al. (2017), the encoding was the concatenation of the embedding of the *definiendum*, a vector representation of its sequence of characters derived from a character-level CNN, and its "hypernym embedding". Gadetsky et al. (2018) used a sigmoid-based gating module to tweak the *definiendum* embedding. The architecture proposed by Chang et al. (2018) is comprised of four modules, only one of which is used as a decoder: the remaining three are meant to convert the *definiendum* as a sparse embedding, select some of the sparse components of its meaning based on a provided context, and encode it into a representation adequate for the decoder.

Aside from theoretical implications, there is another clear gain in considering definition modeling as a sequence-to-sequence task. Recent advances in embedding designs have introduced contextual embeddings (McCann et al., 2017; Peters et al., 2018; Devlin et al., 2018); and these share the particularity that they are a "function of the entire sentence" (Peters et al., 2018): in other words, vector representations are assigned to tokens rather than to word types, and moreover semantic information about a token can be distributed over other token representations. To extend definition modeling to contextual embeddings therefore requires that we devise architectures able to encode a word in its context; in that respect sequence-to-sequence architectures are a natural choice.

A related point is that not all *definienda* are comprised of a single word: multi-word expressions include multiple tokens, yet receive a single definition. Word embedding architectures generally require a pre-processing step to detect these expressions and merge them into a single token. However, as they come with varying degrees of semantic opacity (Cordeiro et al., 2016), a definition modeling system would benefit from directly accessing the tokens they are made up from. Therefore, if we are to address the entirety of the language and the entirety of existing embedding architectures in future studies, reformulating definition modeling as a sequence-to-sequence task becomes a necessity.

## 4 Formalization

A sequence-to-sequence formulation of definition modeling can formally be seen as a mapping between contexts of occurrence of *definienda* and their corresponding definitions. It moreover requires that the *definiendum* be formally distinguished from the remaining context: otherwise the definition could not be linked to any particular word of the contextual sequence, and thus would need to be equally valid for any word of the contextual sequence.

We formalize definition modeling as mapping to sequences of *definientia* from sequences of pairs $\langle w_1, i_1 \rangle, \ldots, \langle w_n, i_n \rangle$, where $w_k$ is the $k^{\text{th}}$ word in the input and $i_k \in \{0, 1\}$ indicates whether the $k^{\text{th}}$ token is to be defined. As only one element of the sequence should be highlighted, we expect the set of all indicators to contain only two elements: the one, $i_d = 1$, to mark the *definiendum*, the other, $i_c = 0$, to mark the context; this entails that we encode this marking using one bit only.[2]

To treat definition modeling as a sequence-to-sequence task, the information from each pair $\langle w_k, i_k \rangle$ has to be integrated into a single repre-

[2]Multiple instances of the same *definiendum* within a single context should all share a single definition, and therefore could theoretically all be marked using the *definiendum* indicator $i_d = 1$. Likewise the words that make up a multi-word expression should all be marked with this $i_d$ indicator. In this work, however, we only mark a single item; in cases when multiple occurrences of the same *definiendum* were attested, we simply marked the first occurrence.

sentation $\vec{marked}_k$:

$$\vec{marked}_k = mark(i_k, \vec{w_k}) \quad (1)$$

This marking function can theoretically take any form. Considering that definition modeling uses the embedding of the definiendum $\vec{w_d} = e(w_d)$, in this work we study a multiplicative and an additive mechanism, as they are conceptually the simplest form this marking can take in a vector space. They are given schematically in Figure 1, and formally defined as:

$$\vec{marked}_k^{\times} = i_k \times \vec{w_k} \quad (2)$$

$$\vec{marked}_k^{+} = e(i_k) + \vec{w_k} \quad (3)$$

The last point to take into account is where to set the marking. Two natural choices are to set it either before or after encoded representations were obtained. We can formalize this using either of the following equation, with $\mathcal{E}$ the model's encoder:

$$\vec{marked}_k^{\text{after}} = mark(i_k, \mathcal{E}(\vec{w_k}))$$

$$\vec{marked}_k^{\text{before}} = \mathcal{E}(mark(i_k, \vec{w_k})) \quad (4)$$

### 4.1 Multiplicative marking: SELECT

The first option we consider is to use scalar multiplication to distinguish the word to define. In such a scenario, the marked token encoding is

$$\vec{marked}_k^{\times} = i_k \times \vec{w_k} \quad (2)$$

As we use bit information as indicators, this form of marking entails that only the representation of the *definiendum* be preserved and that all other contextual representations are set to $\vec{0} = (0, \cdots, 0)$: thus multiplicative marking amounts to selecting just the *definiendum* embedding and discarding other token embeddings. The contextualized *definiendum* encoding bears the trace of its context, but detailed information is irreparably lost. Hence, we refer to such an integration mechanism as a SELECT marking of the *definiendum*.

When to apply marking, as introduced by eq. 4, is crucial when using the multiplicative marking scheme SELECT. Should we mark the *definiendum* before encoding, then only the *definiendum* embedding is passed into the encoder: the resulting system provides out-of-context definitions, like in Noraset et al. (2017) where the definition is not linked to the context of a word but to its *definiendum* only. For context to be taken into account under the multiplicative strategy, tokens $w_k$ must be encoded and contextualized before integration with the indicator $i_k$.

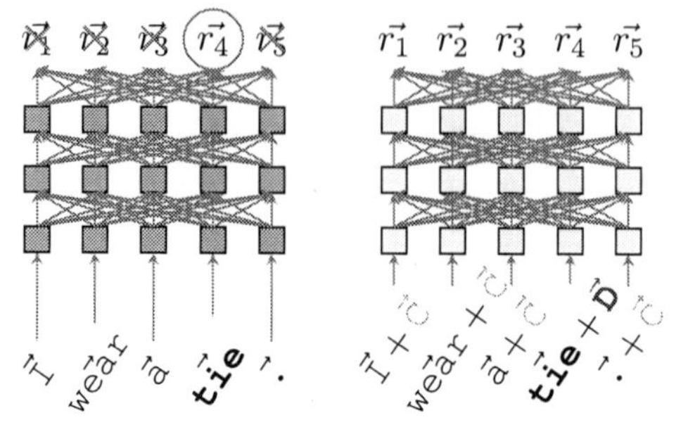

(a) SELECT: Selecting from encoded items. Items are contextualized and the *definiendum* is singled out from them.

(b) ADD: Additive marking in encoder. Context items and *definiendum* are marked by adding dedicated embeddings.

Figure 1: Additive vs. multiplicative integration

Figure 1a presents the contextual SELECT mechanism visually. It consists in coercing the decoder to attend only to the contextualized representation for the *definiendum*. To do so, we encode the full context and then select only the encoded representation of the *definiendum*, dropping the rest of the context, before running the decoder. In the case of the Transformer architecture, this is equivalent to using a multiplicative marking on the encoded representations: vectors that have been zeroed out are ignored during attention and thus cannot influence the behavior of the decoder.

This SELECT approach may seem intuitive and naturally interpretable, as it directly controls what information is passed to the decoder—we carefully select only the contextualized *definiendum*, thus the only remaining zone of uncertainty would be how exactly contextualization is performed. It also seems to provide a strong and reasonable bias for training the definition generation system. Such an approach, however, is not guaranteed to excel: forcibly omitted context could contain important information that might not be easily incorporated in the *definiendum* embedding.

Being simple and natural, the SELECT approach resembles architectures like that of Gadetsky et al. (2018) and Chang et al. (2018): the full encoder is dedicated to altering the embedding of the *definiendum* on the basis of its context; in that, the encoder may be seen as a dedicated contextualization sub-module.

### 4.2 Additive marking: ADD

We also study an additive mechanism shown in Figure 1b (henceforth ADD). It concretely consists in embedding the word $w_k$ and its indicator bit $i_k$ in the same vector space and adding the corresponding vectors:

$$\overrightarrow{marked}_k^{+} = e(i_k) + \vec{w_k} \quad (3)$$

In other words, under ADD we distinguish the *definiendum* by adding a vector $\vec{\mathtt{D}}$ to the *definiendum* embedding, and another vector $\vec{\mathtt{C}}$ to the remaining context token embeddings; both markers $\vec{\mathtt{D}}$ and $\vec{\mathtt{C}}$ are learned during training. In our implementation, markers are added to the input of the encoder, so that the encoder has access to this information; we leave the question of whether to integrate indicators and words at other points of the encoding process, as suggested in eq. 4, to future work.

Additive marking of substantive features has its precedents. For example, BERT embeddings (Devlin et al., 2018) are trained using two sentences at once as input; sentences are distinguished with added markers called "segment encodings". Tokens from the first sentence are all marked with an added vector $\vec{\mathtt{seg}}_A$, whereas tokens from second sentences are all marked with an added vector $\vec{\mathtt{seg}}_B$. The main difference here is that we only mark one item with the marker $\vec{D}$, while all others are marked with $\vec{C}$.

This ADD marking is more expressive than the SELECT architecture. Sequence-to-sequence decoders typically employ an attention to the input source (Bahdanau et al., 2014), which corresponds to a re-weighting of the encoded input sequence based on a similarity between the current state of the decoder (the 'query') and each member of the input sequence (the 'keys'). This re-weighting is normalized with a softmax function, producing a probability distribution over keys. However, both non-contextual definition modeling and the SELECT approach produce singleton encoded sequences: in such scenarios the attention mechanism assigns a single weight of 1 and thus devolves into a simple linear transformation of the value and makes the attention mechanism useless. Using an additive marker, rather than a selective mechanism, will prevent this behavior.

## 5 Evaluation

We implement several sequence to sequence models with the Transformer architecture (Vaswani et al., 2017), building on the OpenNMT library (Klein et al., 2017) with adaptations and modifications when necessary.[3] Throughout this work, we use GloVe vectors (Pennington et al., 2014) and freeze weights of all embeddings for a fairer comparison with previous models; words not in GloVe but observed in train or validation data and missing *definienda* in our test sets were randomly initialized with components drawn from a normal distribution $\mathcal{N}(0, 1)$.

We train a distinct model for each dataset. We batch examples by 8,192, using gradient accumulation to circumvent GPU limitations. We optimize the network using Adam with $\beta_1 = 0.99$, $\beta_2 = 0.998$, a learning rate of 2, label smoothing of 0.1, Noam exponential decay with 2000 warmup steps, and dropout rate of 0.4. The parameters are initialized using Xavier. Models were trained for up to 120,000 steps with checkpoints at each 1000 steps; we stopped training if perplexity on the validation dataset stopped improving. We report results from checkpoints performing best on validation.

### 5.1 Implementation of the Non-contextual Definition Modeling System

In non-contextual definition modeling, *definienda* are mapped directly to definitions. As the source corresponds only to the *definiendum*, we conjecture that few parameters are required for the encoder. We use 1 layer for the encoder, 6 for the decoder, 300 dimensions per hidden representations and 6 heads for multi-head attention. We do not share vocabularies between the encoder and the decoder: therefore output tokens can only correspond to words attested as *definientia*.[4]

The dropout rate and warmup steps number were set using a hyperparameter search on the dataset from Noraset et al. (2017), during which encoder and decoder vocabulary were merged for computational simplicity and models stopped after 12,000 steps. We first fixed dropout to 0.1 and tested warmup step values between 1000 and

[3] Code & data are available at the following URL: https://github.com/TimotheeMickus/onmt-selectrans.

[4] In our case, not sharing vocabularies prevents the model from considering rare words only used as *definienda*, such as "*penumbra*" as potential outputs, and was found to improve performances.

10,000 by increments of 1000, then focused on the most promising span (1000–4000 steps) and exhaustively tested dropout rates from 0.2 to 0.8 by increments of 0.1.

### 5.2 Implementation of Contextualized Definition Modeling Systems

To compare the effects of the two integration strategies that we discussed in section 4, we implement both the additive marking approach (ADD, cf. section 4.2) and the alternative 'encode and select' approach (SELECT, cf. section 4.1). To match with the complex input source, we define encoders with 6 layers; we reemploy the set of hyperparameters previously found for the non-contextual system. Other implementation details, initialization strategies and optimization algorithms are kept the same as described above for the non-contextual version of the model.

We stress that the two approaches we compare for contextualizing the definiendum are applicable to almost any sequence-to-sequence neural architecture with an attention mechanism to the input source.[5] Here we chose to rely on a Transformer-based architecture (Vaswani et al., 2017), which has set the state of the art in a wide range of tasks, from language modeling (Dai et al., 2019) to machine translation (Ott et al., 2018). It is therefore expected that the Transformer architecture will also improve performances for definition modeling, if our arguments for treating it as a sequence to sequence task are on the right track.

### 5.3 Datasets

We train our models on three distinct datasets, which are all borrowed or adapted from previous works on definition modeling. As a consequence, our experiments focus on the English language. The dataset of Noraset et al. (2017) (henceforth $D_{\mathbf{Nor}}$) maps *definienda* to their respective *definientia*, as well as additional information not used here. In the dataset of Gadetsky et al. (2018) (henceforth $D_{\mathbf{Gad}}$), each example consists of a *definiendum*, the *definientia* for one of its meanings and a contextual cue sentence. $D_{\text{Nor}}$ contains on average shorter definitions than $D_{\text{Gad}}$. Definitions in $D_{\text{Nor}}$ have a mean length of 6.6 and a standard deviation of 5.78, whereas those in $D_{\text{Gad}}$ have a mean length of 11.01 and a standard deviation of 6.96.

[5]For best results, the SELECT mechanism should require a bi-directional encoding mechanism.

Chang et al. (2018) stress that the dataset $D_{\text{Gad}}$ includes many examples where the *definiendum* is absent from the associated cue. About half of these cues doe not contain an exact match for the corresponding *definiendum*, but up to 80% contains either an exact match or an inflected form of the *definiendum* according to lemmatization by the NLTK toolkit (Loper and Bird, 2002). To cope with this problematic characteristic, we converted the dataset into the word-in-context format assumed by our model by concatenating the *definiendum* with the cue. To illustrate this, consider the actual input from $D_{\text{Gad}}$ comprised of the *definiendum* "*fool*" and its associated cue "*enough horsing around—let's get back to work!*": to convert this into a single sequence, we simply prepend the *definiendum* to the cue, which results in the sequence "*fool enough horsing around—let's get back to work!*". Hence the input sequences of $D_{Gad}$ do not constitute linguistically coherent sequences, but it does guarantee that our sequence-to-sequence variants have access to the same input as previous models; therefore the inclusion of this dataset in our experiments is intended mainly for comparison with previous architectures. We also note that this conversion procedure entails that our examples have a very regular structure: the word marked as a *definiendum* is always the first word in the input sequence.

Our second strategy was to restrict the dataset by selecting only cues where the *definiendum* (or its inflected form) is present. The curated dataset (henceforth $D_{\mathbf{Ctx}}$) contains 78,717 training examples, 9,413 for validation and 9,812 for testing. In each example, the first occurrence of the *definiendum* is annotated as such. $D_{\text{Ctx}}$ thus differs from $D_{\text{Gad}}$ in two ways: some definitions have been removed, and the exact citation forms of the *definienda* are not given. Models trained on $D_{\text{Ctx}}$ implicitly need to lemmatize the *definiendum*, since inflected variants of a given word are to be aligned to a common representation; thus they are not directly comparable with models trained with the citation form of the *definiendum* that solely use context as a cue—viz. Gadetsky et al. (2018) & Chang et al. (2018). All this makes $D_{\text{Ctx}}$ harder, but at the same time closer to a realistic application than the other two datasets, since each word appears inflected and in a specific *sentential context*. For applications of definition modeling, it would only be beneficial to take up these challenges; for example, the output "*monotremes: plural of monotreme*"[6] would not have been self-contained, necessitating a second query for "*monotreme*".

### 5.4 Results

We use perplexity, a standard metric in definition modeling, to evaluate and compare our models. Informally, perplexity assesses the model's confidence in producing the ground-truth output when presented the source input. It is formally defined as the exponentiation of cross-entropy. We do not report BLEU or ROUGE scores due to the fact that an important number of ground-truth definitions are comprised of a single word, in particular in $D_{\text{Nor}}$ ($\approx 25\%$). Single word outputs can either be assessed as entirely correct or entirely wrong using BLEU or ROUGE. However consider for instance the word "*elation*": that it be defined either as "*mirth*" or "*joy*" should only influence our metric slightly, and not be discounted as a completely wrong prediction.

| | $D_{\text{Nor}}$ | $D_{\text{Gad}}$ | $D_{\text{Ctx}}$ |
|---|---|---|---|
| Noraset et al. | 48.168 | 45.620 | – |
| Gadetsky et al. | – | 43.540 | – |
| Non-contextual | 42.199 | 39.428 | 48.266 |
| ADD | – | 33.678 | 43.695 |
| SELECT | – | 33.998 | 62.039 |

Table 1: Results (perplexity)

Table 1 describes our main results in terms of perplexity. We do not compare with Chang et al. (2018), as they did not report the perplexity of their system and focused on a different dataset; likewise, Yang et al. (2019) consider only the Chinese variant of the task. Perplexity measures for Noraset et al. (2017) and Gadetsky et al. (2018) are taken from the authors' respective publications.

All our models perform better than previous proposals, by a margin of 4 to 10 points, for a relative improvement of 11–23%. Part of this improvement may be due to our use of Transformer-based architectures (Vaswani et al., 2017), which is known to perform well on semantic tasks (Radford, 2018; Cer et al., 2018; Devlin et al., 2018; Radford et al., 2019, eg.). Like Gadetsky et al. (2018), we conclude that disambiguating the *definiendum*, when done correctly, improves performances: our best performing contextual model outranks the non-contextual variant by 5 to 6 points. The marking of the definiendum out of its context (ADD vs. SELECT) also impacts results. Note also that we do not rely on task-specific external resources (unlike Noraset et al., 2017; Yang et al., 2019) or on pre-training (unlike Gadetsky et al., 2018).

Our contextual systems trained on the $D_{\text{Gad}}$ dataset used the concatenation of the *definiendum* and the contextual cue as inputs. The definiendum was always at the start of the training example. This regular structure has shown to be useful for the models' performance: all models perform significantly worse on the more realistic data of $D_{\text{Ctx}}$ than on $D_{\text{Gad}}$. The $D_{\text{Ctx}}$ dataset is intrinsically harder for other reasons as well: it requires some form of lemmatization in every three out of eight training examples, and contains less data than other datasets, only half as many examples as $D_{\text{Nor}}$, and 20% less than $D_{\text{Gad}}$.

The surprisingly poor results of SELECT on the $D_{\text{Ctx}}$ dataset may be partially blamed on the absence of a regular structure in $D_{\text{Ctx}}$. Unlike $D_{\text{Gad}}$, where the model must only learn to contextualize the first element of the sequence, in $D_{\text{Ctx}}$ the model has to single out the *definiendum* which may appear anywhere in the sentence. Any information stored only in representations of contextual tokens will be lost to the decoders. The SELECT model therefore suffers of a bottleneck, which is highly regular in $D_{\text{Gad}}$ and that it may therefore learn to cope with; however predicting *where* in the input sequence the bottleneck will appear is far from trivial in the $D_{\text{Ctx}}$ dataset. We also attempted to retrain this model with various settings of hyperparameters, modifying dropout rate, number of warmup steps, and number of layers in the encoder—but to no avail. An alternative explanation may be that in the case of the $D_{\text{Gad}}$ dataset, the regular structure of the input entails that the first positional encoding is used as an additive marking device: only *definienda* are marked with the positional encoding $\vec{\text{pos}}(1)$, and thus the architecture does not purely embrace a selective approach but a mixed one.

In any event, even on the $D_{\text{Gad}}$ dataset where the margin is very small, the perplexity of the additive marking approach ADD is better than that of the SELECT model. This lends empirical support to our claim that definition modeling is a non-trivial sequence-to-sequence task, which can be

[6] Definition from Wiktionary.

better treated with sequence methods. The stability of the performance improvement over the non-contextual variant in both contextual datasets also highlights that our proposed additive marking is fairly robust, and functions equally well when confronted to somewhat artificial inputs, as in $D_{\text{Gad}}$, or to linguistically coherent sequences, as in $D_{\text{Ctx}}$.

## 6 Qualitative Analysis

| | |
|---|---|
| **filch** | to seize |
| **grammar** | the science of language |
| **implosion** | a sudden and violent collapse |

(a) Handpicked sample

| | |
|---|---|
| **sediment** | to percolate |
| **deputation** | the act of inciting |
| **ancestry** | lineage |

(b) Random sample

Table 2: Examples of production (non-contextual model trained on $D_{\text{Nor}}$)

A manual analysis of definitions produced by our system reveals issues similar to those discussed by Noraset et al. (2017), namely self-reference,[7] POS-mismatches, over- and under-specificity, antonymy, and incoherence. Annotating distinct productions from the validation set, for the non-contextual model trained on $D_{\text{Nor}}$, we counted 9.9% of self-references, 11.6% POS-mismatches, and 1.3% of words defined as their antonyms. We counted POS-mismatches whenever the definition seemed to fit another part-of-speech than that of the *definiendum*, regardless of both of their meanings; cf. Table 2 for examples.

For comparison, we annotated the first 1000 productions of the validation set from our ADD model trained on $D_{\text{Ctx}}$. We counted 18.4% POS mismatches and 4.4% of self-referring definitions; examples are shown in Table 3. The higher rate of POS-mismatch may be due to the model's hardship in finding which word is to be defined since the model is not presented with the *definiendum* alone: access to the full context may confuse it. On the other hand, the lower number of self-referring definitions may also be linked to this richer, more varied input: this would allow the model not to fall back on simply reusing the *definiendum* as its own *definiens*. Self-referring definitions highlight that our models equate the meaning of the *definiendum* to the composed meaning of its *definientia*. Simply masking the corresponding output embedding might suffice to prevent this specific problem; preliminary experiments in that direction suggest that this may also help decrease perplexity further.

As for POS-mismatches, we do note that the work of Noraset et al. (2017) had a much lower rate of 4.29%: we suggest that this may be due to the fact that they employ a learned character-level convolutional network, which arguably would be able to capture orthography and rudiments of morphology. Adding such a sub-module to our proposed architecture might diminish the number of mistagged *definienda*. Another possibility would be to pre-train the model, as was done by Gadetsky et al. (2018): in our case in particular, the encoder could be trained for POS-tagging or lemmatization.

Lastly, one important kind of mistakes we observed is hallucinations. Consider for instance this production by the ADD model trained on $D_{\text{Ctx}}$, for the word "*beta*": "*the twentieth letter of the Greek alphabet (κ), transliterated as 'o'.*". Nearly everything it contains is factually wrong, though the general semantics are close enough to deceive an unaware reader.[8] We conjecture that filtering out hallucinatory productions will be a main challenge for future definition modeling architectures, for two main reasons: firstly, the tools and metrics necessary to assess and handle such hallucinations have yet to be developed; secondly, the input given to the system being word embeddings, research will be faced with the problem of grounding these distributional representations—how can we ensure that "*beta*" is correctly defined as "*the second letter of the Greek alphabet, transliterated as 'b'*", if we only have access to a representation derived from its contexts of usage? Integration of word embeddings with structured knowledge bases might be needed for accurate treatment of such cases.

[7] Self-referring definitions are those where a *definiendum* is used as a *definiens* for itself. Dictionaries are expected to be exempt of such definitions: as readers are assumed not to know the meaning of the *definiendum* when looking it up.

[8] On a related note, other examples were found to contain unwanted social biases; consider the production by the same model for the word "*blackface*": "*relating to or characteristic of the theatre*". Part of the social bias here may be blamed on the under-specific description that omits the offensive nature of the word; however contrast the definition of Merriam Webster for *blackface*, which includes a note on the offensiveness of the term, with that of Wiktionary, which does not. Cf. Bolukbasi et al. (2016); Swinger et al. (2018) for a discussion on biases within embedding themselves.

| Error type | Context (*definiendum* in bold) | Production |
|---|---|---|
| POS-mismatch | her **major** is linguistics | most important or important |
| Self-reference | he wrote a letter of **apology** to the hostess | a formal expression of apology |

Table 3: Examples of common errors (ADD model trained on $D_{\mathrm{Nor}}$)

## 7 Conclusion

We introduced an approach to generating word definitions that allows the model to access rich contextual information about the word token to be defined. Building on the distributional hypothesis, we naturally treat definition generation as a sequence-to-sequence task of mapping the word's context of usage (input sequence) into the context-appropriate definition (output sequence).

We showed that our approach is competitive against a more naive 'contextualize and select' pipeline. This was demonstrated by comparison both to the previous contextualized model by Gadetsky et al. (2018) and to the Transformer-based SELECT variation of our model, which differs from the proposed architecture only in the context encoding pipeline. While our results are encouraging, given the existing benchmarks we were limited to perplexity measurements in our quantitative evaluation. A more nuanced semantically driven methodology might be useful in the future to better assess the merits of our system in comparison to alternatives.

Our model opens several avenues of future explorations. One could straightforwardly extend it to generate definitions of multiword expressions or phrases, or to analyze vector compositionality models by generating paraphrases for vector representations produced by these algorithms. Another strength of our approach is that it can provide the basis for a standardized benchmark for contextualized and non-contextual embeddings alike: downstream evaluation tasks for embeddings systems in general either apply to non-contextual embeddings (Gladkova et al., 2016, eg.) or to contextual embeddings (Wang et al., 2019, eg.) exclusively, redefining definition modeling as a sequence-to-sequence task will allow in future works to compare models using contextual and non-contextual embeddings in a unified fashion. Lastly, we also intend to experiment on languages other than English, especially considering that the required resources for our model only amount to a set of pretrained embeddings and a dataset of definitions, either of which are generally simple to obtain.

While there is a potential for local improvements, our approach has demonstrated its ability to account for contextualized word meaning in a principled way, while training contextualized token encoding and definition generation end-to-end. Our implementation is efficient and fast, building on free open source libraries for deep learning, and shows good empirical results. Our code, trained models, and data will be made available to the community.

## Acknowledgments

We thank Quentin Gliosca for his many remarks throughout all stages of this project. We also thanks Kees van Deemter, as well as anonymous reviewers, for their thoughtful criticism of this work. The work was supported by a public grant overseen by the French National Research Agency (ANR) as part of the "Investissements d'Avenir" program: Idex *Lorraine Université d'Excellence* (reference: ANR-15-IDEX-0004).

## References

Sanjeev Arora, Yuanzhi Li, Yingyu Liang, Tengyu Ma, and Andrej Risteski. 2018. Linear algebraic structure of word senses, with applications to polysemy. *Transactions of the Association for Computational Linguistics*, 6:483–495.

Dzmitry Bahdanau, Kyunghyun Cho, and Yoshua Bengio. 2014. Neural machine translation by jointly learning to align and translate. *CoRR*, abs/1409.0473.

Sergey Bartunov, Dmitry Kondrashkin, Anton Osokin, and Dmitry P. Vetrov. 2016. Breaking sticks and ambiguities with adaptive skip-gram. In *Proceedings of the 19th International Conference on Artificial Intelligence and Statistics, AISTATS 2016, Cadiz, Spain, May 9-11, 2016*, pages 130–138.

Miroslav Batchkarov, Thomas Kober, Jeremy Reffin, Julie Weeds, and David Weir. 2016. A critique of word similarity as a method for evaluating distributional semantic models. In *Proceedings of the 1st Workshop on Evaluating Vector-Space Representations for NLP*, pages 7–12, Berlin, Germany. Association for Computational Linguistics.

Gemma Boleda. 2019. Distributional semantics and linguistic theory. *CoRR*, abs/1905.01896.

Tolga Bolukbasi, Kai-Wei Chang, James Y Zou, Venkatesh Saligrama, and Adam T Kalai. 2016. Man is to computer programmer as woman is to homemaker? debiasing word embeddings. In D. D. Lee, M. Sugiyama, U. V. Luxburg, I. Guyon, and R. Garnett, editors, *Advances in Neural Information Processing Systems 29*, pages 4349–4357. Curran Associates, Inc.

Tom Bosc and Pascal Vincent. 2018. Auto-encoding dictionary definitions into consistent word embeddings. In *Proceedings of the 2018 Conference on Empirical Methods in Natural Language Processing*, pages 1522–1532. Association for Computational Linguistics.

Daniel Cer, Yinfei Yang, Sheng-yi Kong, Nan Hua, Nicole Limtiaco, Rhomni St. John, Noah Constant, Mario Guajardo-Cespedes, Steve Yuan, Chris Tar, Yun-Hsuan Sung, Brian Strope, and Ray Kurzweil. 2018. Universal sentence encoder. *CoRR*, abs/1803.11175.

Ting-Yun Chang, Ta-Chung Chi, Shang-Chi Tsai, and Yun-Nung Chen. 2018. xsense: Learning sense-separated sparse representations and textual definitions for explainable word sense networks. *CoRR*, abs/1809.03348.

Silvio Cordeiro, Carlos Ramisch, Marco Idiart, and Aline Villavicencio. 2016. Predicting the compositionality of nominal compounds: Giving word embeddings a hard time. In *Proceedings of the 54th Annual Meeting of the Association for Computational Linguistics (Volume 1: Long Papers)*, pages 1986–1997, Berlin, Germany. ACL. CORE2018 rank: A*. `https://aclweb.org/anthology/P16-1187`.

Zihang Dai, Zhilin Yang, Yiming Yang, Jaime G. Carbonell, Quoc V. Le, and Ruslan Salakhutdinov. 2019. Transformer-xl: Attentive language models beyond a fixed-length context. *CoRR*, abs/1901.02860.

Jacob Devlin, Ming-Wei Chang, Kenton Lee, and Kristina Toutanova. 2018. BERT: pre-training of deep bidirectional transformers for language understanding. *CoRR*, abs/1810.04805.

J.R. Firth. 1957. *Papers in linguistics, 1934-1951*. Oxford University Press.

Artyom Gadetsky, Ilya Yakubovskiy, and Dmitry Vetrov. 2018. Conditional generators of words definitions. In *Proceedings of the 56th Annual Meeting of the Association for Computational Linguistics (Volume 2: Short Papers)*, pages 266–271. Association for Computational Linguistics.

Anna Gladkova, Aleksandr Drozd, and Satoshi Matsuoka. 2016. Analogy-based detection of morphological and semantic relations with word embeddings: what works and what doesn't. In *SRWHLT-NAACL*.

Zellig Harris. 1954. Distributional structure. *Word*, 10(23):146–162.

Felix Hill, Kyunghyun Cho, and Anna Korhonen. 2016. Learning distributed representations of sentences from unlabelled data. *CoRR*, abs/1602.03483.

G. Klein, Y. Kim, Y. Deng, J. Senellart, and A. M. Rush. 2017. OpenNMT: Open-Source Toolkit for Neural Machine Translation. *ArXiv e-prints*.

Angeliki Lazaridou, Marco Arturo Marelli, and Marco Baroni. 2017. Multimodal word meaning induction from minimal exposure to natural text. *Cognitive science*, 41 Suppl 4:677–705.

Alessandro Lenci. 2018. Distributional models of word meaning. *Annual review of Linguistics*, 4:151–171.

Omer Levy and Yoav Goldberg. 2014a. Linguistic regularities in sparse and explicit word representations. In *Proceedings of the Eighteenth Conference on Computational Natural Language Learning*, pages 171–180. Association for Computational Linguistics.

Omer Levy and Yoav Goldberg. 2014b. Neural word embedding as implicit matrix factorization. In Z. Ghahramani, M. Welling, C. Cortes, N. D. Lawrence, and K. Q. Weinberger, editors, *Advances in Neural Information Processing Systems 27*, pages 2177–2185. Curran Associates, Inc.

Edward Loper and Steven Bird. 2002. Nltk: The natural language toolkit. In *In Proceedings of the ACL Workshop on Effective Tools and Methodologies for Teaching Natural Language Processing and Computational Linguistics. Philadelphia: Association for Computational Linguistics*.

Bryan McCann, James Bradbury, Caiming Xiong, and Richard Socher. 2017. Learned in translation: Contextualized word vectors. *CoRR*, abs/1708.00107.

Thanapon Noraset, Chen Liang, Lawrence Birnbaum, and Doug Downey. 2017. Definition modeling: Learning to define word embeddings in natural language. In *AAAI*.

Myle Ott, Sergey Edunov, David Grangier, and Michael Auli. 2018. Scaling neural machine translation. *CoRR*, abs/1806.00187.

Jeffrey Pennington, Richard Socher, and Christopher D. Manning. 2014. Glove: Global vectors for word representation. In *Proceedings of the 2014 Conference on Empirical Methods in Natural Language Processing (EMNLP)*.

Matthew E. Peters, Mark Neumann, Mohit Iyyer, Matt Gardner, Christopher Clark, Kenton Lee, and Luke Zettlemoyer. 2018. Deep contextualized word representations. In *Proc. of NAACL*.

Alec Radford. 2018. Improving language understanding by generative pre-training.

Alec Radford, Jeff Wu, Rewon Child, David Luan, Dario Amodei, and Ilya Sutskever. 2019. Language models are unsupervised multitask learners.

Nathaniel Swinger, Maria De-Arteaga, Neil Thomas Heffernan IV, Mark D. M. Leiserson, and Adam Tauman Kalai. 2018. What are the biases in my word embedding? *CoRR*, abs/1812.08769.

Wilson Taylor. 1953. Cloze procedure: A new tool for measuring readability. *Journalism Quarterly*, 30:415–433.

Julien Tissier, Christophe Gravier, and Amaury Habrard. 2017. Dict2vec : Learning word embeddings using lexical dictionaries. In *EMNLP*.

Ashish Vaswani, Noam Shazeer, Niki Parmar, Jakob Uszkoreit, Llion Jones, Aidan N Gomez, Ł ukasz Kaiser, and Illia Polosukhin. 2017. Attention is all you need. In I. Guyon, U. V. Luxburg, S. Bengio, H. Wallach, R. Fergus, S. Vishwanathan, and R. Garnett, editors, *Advances in Neural Information Processing Systems 30*, pages 5998–6008. Curran Associates, Inc.

Alex Wang, Amanpreet Singh, Julian Michael, Felix Hill, Omer Levy, and Samuel R. Bowman. 2019. GLUE: A multi-task benchmark and analysis platform for natural language understanding. In the Proceedings of ICLR.

Tong Wang, Abdelrahman Mohamed, and Graeme Hirst. 2015. Learning lexical embeddings with syntactic and lexicographic knowledge. In *Proceedings of the 53rd Annual Meeting of the Association for Computational Linguistics and the 7th International Joint Conference on Natural Language Processing (Volume 2: Short Papers)*, pages 458–463. Association for Computational Linguistics.

Liner Yang, Cunliang Kong, Yun Chen, Yang Liu, Qinan Fan, and Erhong Yang. 2019. Incorporating sememes into chinese definition modeling. *CoRR*, abs/1905.06512.

# Improving Semantic Dependency Parsing with Syntactic Features

**Robin Kurtz, Daniel Roxbo, Marco Kuhlmann**

Linköping University
Department of Computer and Information Science
robin.kurtz@liu.se, marco.kuhlmann@liu.se

## Abstract

We extend a state-of-the-art deep neural architecture for semantic dependency parsing with features defined over syntactic dependency trees. Our empirical results show that only gold-standard syntactic information leads to consistent improvements in semantic parsing accuracy, and that the magnitude of these improvements varies with the specific combination of the syntactic and the semantic representation used. In contrast, automatically predicted syntax does not seem to help semantic parsing. Our error analysis suggests that there is a significant overlap between syntactic and semantic representations.

## 1 Introduction

Semantic dependency parsing (SDP) is the task of mapping a sentence into a formal representation of its meaning in the form of a directed graph with arcs between pairs of words. Ever since the release of the now-standard datasets for this task (Oepen et al., 2014, 2015), most of the approaches to semantic dependency parsing have been based on previous and ongoing work in syntactic parsing. In particular, several semantic parsers make use of features defined over syntactic dependency trees; one recent example is the system of Peng et al. (2018).

In this paper we study to what extent semantic dependency parsing actually benefits from syntactic features. More specifically, we carry out experiments to identify those combinations of semantic and syntactic representations that yield the highest parsing accuracy. This is interesting not only for parser developers – using improvement or non-improvement in parsing accuracy as an indicator, our study also contributes to a better understanding of the similarities and contentful differences between semantic and syntactic representations.

Semantic dependency parsers are typically conceptualized as systems for structured prediction, combining a data-driven component that learns how to score dependency graphs with a decoder that retrieves one or several highest-scoring target graphs from the exponentially large search space of candidate graphs. Among decoding algorithms we find approaches based on integer linear programming (Almeida and Martins, 2015; Peng et al., 2017), dynamic programming algorithms that support exact decoding for restricted classes of graphs (Kuhlmann and Jonsson, 2015; Cao et al., 2017), and transition-based approaches introducing new shift–reduce-style automata (Zhang et al., 2016; Wang et al., 2018). Regarding the learning component, state-of-the-art parsing results have been achieved using neural architectures (Peng et al., 2017; Wang et al., 2018; Dozat and Manning, 2018). The system of Dozat and Manning (2018) even draws essentially all of its strength from its neural core, employing a trivial decoder. The parser used in this paper is a (slightly modified) re-implementation of that system developed by Roxbo (2019), which adds syntactic information via a simple head feature, along the lines of Peng et al. (2018).

*Paper Structure.* After providing some background in Section 2, we describe the architecture of our parser in Section 3, and our data and experimental setup in Section 4. In Section 5 we present our empirical results and complement them with an error analysis in Section 6. Section 7 concludes the paper and provides an outlook on future work.

## 2 Background

In both semantic and syntactic dependency parsing, the target structures are directed graphs with lexicalized nodes and bilexical arcs. More formally, a *dependency graph* for a sentence $\boldsymbol{x} = x_1, \dots, x_n$ is an arc-labelled directed graph whose nodes are in

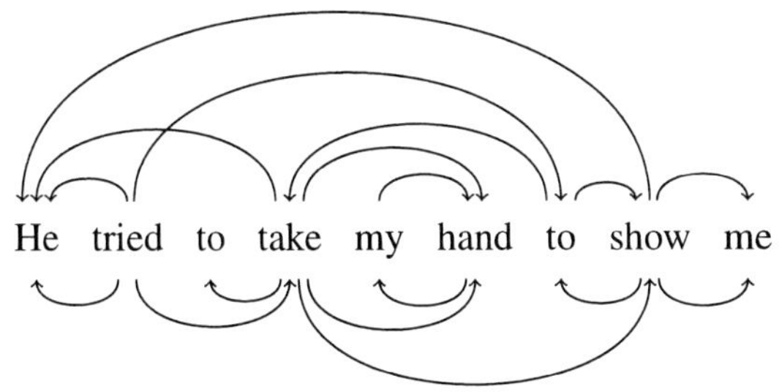


Figure 1: A sample sentence with a gold-standard semantic dependency graph in the DM representation (Flickinger et al., 2016, #41526060) (upper half-plane) and a predicted syntactic dependency tree in the Stanford Basic representation (lower half-plane). (Arc labels omitted in this example.)

one-to-one correspondence to the tokens of $\boldsymbol{x}$. For an arc $i \rightarrow j$ we refer to the nodes $i$ and $j$ as *head* and *dependent*, respectively. We follow standard conventions and visualize dependency graphs with their nodes laid out on a line according to the linear order of the sentence, and their arcs drawn in the half-plane above (or sometimes below) the nodes. An example graph is provided in Figure 1.

In syntactic dependency parsing, target representations are restricted to trees. Formally, a *dependency tree* is a dependency graph that is connected, acyclic, and such that each node except a distinguished root node has at most one incoming arc. The root node has no incoming arc. In a dependency tree we write $h(i)$ to denote the head of the incoming arc to the (non-root) node $i$.

## 3 Parser

We now give a compact description of our parser, a version of the system of Dozat and Manning (2018); for more details, we refer to Roxbo (2019). We use essentially the same architecture for semantic parsing and for predicting the trees over which we define our syntactic features.

### 3.1 Neural Network Model

The core of our parser is a bidirectional recurrent neural network with Long Short-Term Memory cells (BiLSTM; Hochreiter and Schmidhuber, 1997). Feeding this network with a sentence $\boldsymbol{x} = x_1, \dots, x_n$ in the form of a sequence of (initially random) word embeddings $\boldsymbol{w}_i$, we obtain a sequence of context-dependent embeddings $\mathbf{c}_i$:

$$\boldsymbol{c}_1, \dots, \boldsymbol{c}_n = \text{BiLSTM}(\boldsymbol{w}_1, \dots, \boldsymbol{w}_n)$$

The word embeddings can be easily augmented by additional lexical features, such as pre-trained word embeddings or embeddings for part-of-speech tags or lemmas. In this study we add embeddings created via character-based LSTMs and 100-dimensional GloVe (Pennington et al., 2014) embeddings.

The network processes the contextual token embeddings $\boldsymbol{c}_i$ by two parallel feedforward neural networks (FNN), which are meant to learn specialized representations for the potential roles of each word as head and dependent:

$$\boldsymbol{h}_i = \text{FNN}_h(\boldsymbol{c}_i) \qquad \boldsymbol{d}_i = \text{FNN}_d(\boldsymbol{c}_i)$$

These embeddings are then used to score each potential arc $i \rightarrow j$ via a bilinear model with weight matrix $\boldsymbol{U}$ that will be learned during training:

$$\text{score}(\boldsymbol{h}_i, \boldsymbol{d}_j) = \boldsymbol{h}_i^\top \boldsymbol{U} \boldsymbol{d}_j$$

### 3.2 Decoding

The matrix of arc scores can be processed by any type of arc-factored decoder to return the highest-scoring graph for the complete sentence. Our semantic parser greedily selects all arcs with a non-negative score. The syntactic parser uses the Chu–Liu/Edmonds (CLE) maximum spanning tree algorithm (Chu and Liu, 1965; Edmonds, 1967) implemented in Uniparse (Varab and Schluter, 2018).

### 3.3 Adding Labels

To predict labelled arcs, we take two different approaches: The semantic parser computes, for each token pair, scores for all potential labels, including a special NONE label that represents the absence of an arc between the two tokens; this yields a three-dimensional score tensor rather than a score matrix. The syntactic parser factorizes the computation and predicts a label for each token pair independently of the arc scorer; this label is only used if an arc is actually selected by the decoder.

### 3.4 Adding Syntactic Features

To add syntactic features to our semantic parser, we follow the same simple approach as Peng et al. (2018): Before feeding the contextual embedding of each token to the arc- and label-scoring components, we extend it with the contextual embedding of its syntactic head in the dependency tree:

$$\boldsymbol{c}'_i = [\boldsymbol{c}_i; \boldsymbol{c}_{h(i)}]$$

This simple variation has a minimal impact on the complexity of the overall model, and makes further analysis and comparison more straightforward.

| Parameter | Value |
|---|---|
| Embeddings | 100 |
| Char LSTM | 1 @ 400 |
| Char linear | 100 |
| BiLSTM | 3 @ 600 |
| Arc/Label FNN | 600 |
| Epochs | 100 |
| Mini-batch size | 50 |
| Adam $\beta_1$ | 0 |
| Adam $\beta_2$ | 0.95 |
| Learning rate | $1 \cdot 10^{-3}$ |
| Gradient clipping | 5 |
| Interpolation constant | 0.025 |
| $L_2$ regularization | $3 \cdot 10^{-9}$ |

Table 1: Network sizes and training parameters.

### 3.5 Training

We train our parser with the Adam optimizer (Kingma and Ba, 2014) and mini-batching. To train the arc and label scorers, we use a binary and a softmax cross-entropy loss, respectively. In the factorized approach used by the syntactic parser, the arc- and label-specific losses are summed up to an overall loss, weighted by an interpolation constant to emphasize the arc scorer:

$$\text{loss}_{\text{total}} = (1 - 0.025) \cdot \text{loss}_{\text{arc}} + 0.025 \cdot \text{loss}_{\text{label}}$$

Due to the size of the model and its fairly large number of trainable parameters (see Table 1), it is prone to overfitting. To address this, we apply equally large dropout rates to nearly all parts of the model (see Table 2). We apply variational dropout (Gal and Ghahramani, 2016) sharing the same dropout mask between all time steps in a sequence. On the LSTM hidden states we use DropConnect (Wan et al., 2013; Merity et al., 2017), a more general variant of dropout which drops individual connections instead of complete nodes of the computation graph.

| Substructure | Rate |
|---|---|
| Embeddings | 20% |
| Char LSTM feedforward | 33% |
| Char LSTM recurrent | 33% |
| Char Linear | 33% |
| BiLSTM feedforward | 45% |
| BiLSTM recurrent | 25% |
| Arc FNN | 25% |
| Arc scorer | 25% |
| Label FNN | 33% |
| Label scorer | 33% |

Table 2: Dropout rates.

## 4 Method

In this section we describe our data and the setup of our experiments.

### 4.1 Data

The main dataset for our experiments is the English part of the standard SDP distribution (Flickinger et al., 2016), which contains semantic dependency graphs for Sections 00–21 of the venerable Penn Treebank (Marcus et al., 1993) in a predefined train/test split, as well as graphs for out-of-domain test sentences from the Brown Corpus (Francis and Kučera, 1985). The graphs come in four different representation types, of which we use three: graphs derived from DeepBank (DM, Oepen and Lønning, 2006; Ivanova et al., 2012); predicate–argument structures computed by the Enju parser (PAS, Miyao, 2006); and graphs derived from the tectogrammatical layer of the Prague Dependency Treebank (PSD, Hajic et al., 2012). Due to their structural differences, the three graph types are more or less difficult to parse into; PSD graphs, for example, feature a considerably larger label inventory than the other types.

The graphs in the SDP dataset come with different types of gold-standard syntactic analyses, of which we use Stanford Basic Dependencies (SB, de Marneffe and Manning, 2008), derived from the Penn Treebank, and DELPH-IN Syntactic Derivation Trees (DT, Ivanova et al., 2012), derived from DeepBank. In addition to those we also use the English Web Treebank (EWT) from the Universal Dependencies (UD) project (Nivre et al., 2017), which contains syntactic dependency trees for text that does not overlap with the SDP data. We note that the EWT is considerably smaller than the SDP dataset.

### 4.2 Experimental Setup

We train three types of semantic dependency parsing models: no syntactic features (N), features extracted from gold-standard syntax trees (G), and features extracted from predicted syntax trees (P). The models of type N serve as our baseline and perform on par with the parser of Dozat and Manning (2018). For models of type G we use gold trees as inputs both during training and at test time; for models of type P, at test time we instead feed the parser with trees predicted by our syntactic parser. For the EWT models we use predicted trees during both training and testing.

| Dataset | Our parser | | StanfordNLP | | UDPipe |
|---|---|---|---|---|---|
| | id | ood | id | ood | |
| SB | 93.2 | 89.9 | 94.2 | 90.9 | |
| DT | 94.0 | 90.3 | 94.9 | 91.7 | |
| EWT | 85.9 | | | | 85.4 |

Table 3: Parsing accuracy for our syntactic models on the in-domain (id) and out-of-domain (ood) test sets for the SDP data, and the regular test set for the EWT data.

Our three syntactic models (for SB, DT, and EWT) were trained using the same architecture and specifications as the semantic models, but use the factorized approach with CLE-decoding instead. Their accuracy is reported in Table 3, with additional results from StanfordNLP (Qi et al., 2018) and UDPipe (Straka and Straková, 2017) for reference. We note that in contrast to those systems' results, ours were achieved without gold POS tags.

## 5 Empirical Results

The results for our semantic dependency parsing models for the three graph types in the SDP dataset are presented in Table 4. For comparison, we add results reported by Dozat and Manning (2018) and Peng et al. (2018), and emphasize for each test set the overall best-performing model.

**Baseline** Our baseline using no syntactic features performs comparable to the systems of Dozat and Manning (2018) and Peng et al. (2018). We note that the results reported for Dozat and Manning (2018) are for models that not only use character embeddings (which we also use), but also part-of-speech tag embeddings (which we do not use).[1] The results reported for Peng et al. (2018) are for models that use predicted syntax. The slight advantage of our baseline over the latter models suggests that the network architecture can provide the same benefits as additional syntactic information.

**Contribution of Syntactic Structure** Looking at the results for the models informed by gold-standard syntax, we see consistent gains in both in-domain and out-of-domain settings, with substantial improvements of 3.1 labelled F1 points for DM–DT, and 2.2 points for PAS–SB. The models informed by predicted syntax, on the other hand, do not achieve any significant improvements over the baseline, and in several cases actually perform slightly worse than it. We saw the same trend in additional experiments (not reported here) where we used predicted trees even during training. Interestingly, while the baseline and the models using predicted syntax have similar F-scores, for the latter we observe a reduction of the number of false negatives (i.e., missing arcs), but also an increase in the number of false positives (i.e., incorrectly predicted arcs). The models using EWT trees do not outperform the baseline, and we omit their further investigation from the rest of the paper.

[1]The best-performing model of Dozat and Manning (2018) additionally uses lemma embeddings.

## 6 Error Analysis

To gain a deeper understanding for our empirical results, we complement them with an error analysis. For space reasons we will focus our analysis on the DM models (Figures 2a–2c); however, we will also discuss results from one PAS model (Figure 2d).

### 6.1 Error Types

Our analysis is based on a two-dimensional classification of errors. In the first dimension, for each semantic parsing model $M$, we break down all errors relative to the no-syntax baseline model into the following four types:

1. false negatives of the baseline avoided by $M$
2. false positives of the baseline avoided by $M$
3. false negatives of $M$ avoided by the baseline
4. false positives of $M$ avoided by the baseline

Type 1 thus consists of arcs that the baseline incorrectly does not and the syntax-informed model $M$ correctly does predict, and so on.

In the second dimension, for each error type we distinguish four different sub-categories, based on the correspondence between the incorrectly predicted/not predicted arc $i \rightarrow j$ in the semantic graph and the structural relation between the head $i$ and dependent $j$ in the syntactic dependency tree:

(a) the dependency tree has an arc $i \rightarrow j$

(b) the dependency tree has an arc $j \rightarrow i$

(c) $i$ and $j$ are siblings in the dependency tree

(d) none of the above

This subclassification allows us to see if there are systematic correspondences between semantic and syntactic relations, and to assess the impact of syntactic features on the semantic parser's ability to handle *difficult* arcs.

| Model | | DM | | PAS | | PSD | |
|---|---|---|---|---|---|---|---|
| | | id | ood | id | ood | id | ood |
| N – no syntax (baseline) | | 92.1 | 87.4 | 92.6 | 89.7 | 79.7 | 77.3 |
| DT | G – gold syntax | **95.2** | **90.9** | 93.2 | 90.3 | 80.0 | 78.3 |
| | P – predicted syntax | 92.2 | 89.3 | 92.4 | 88.9 | 79.5 | 77.5 |
| SB | G – gold syntax | 92.7 | 88.1 | **94.8** | **92.1** | 80.4 | **79.0** |
| | P – predicted syntax | 92.0 | 87.0 | 92.4 | 88.9 | 79.6 | 77.2 |
| EWT | P – predicted syntax | 91.8 | 87.1 | 92.7 | 89.3 | 79.6 | 77.3 |
| Dozat and Manning (2018) | | 92.7 | 87.8 | 94.0 | 90.6 | **80.5** | 78.6 |
| Peng et al. (2018) | | 91.6 | 86.7 | | | 78.9 | 77.1 |

Table 4: Labeled F1 for our semantic parsers on the in-domain (id) and out-of-domain (ood) test sets.

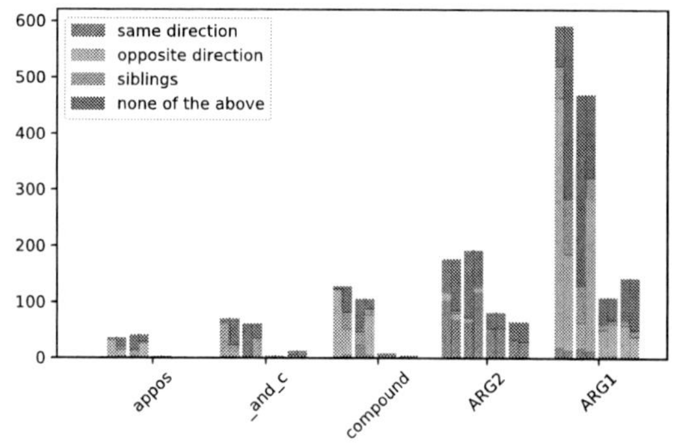


(a) DM + gold DT

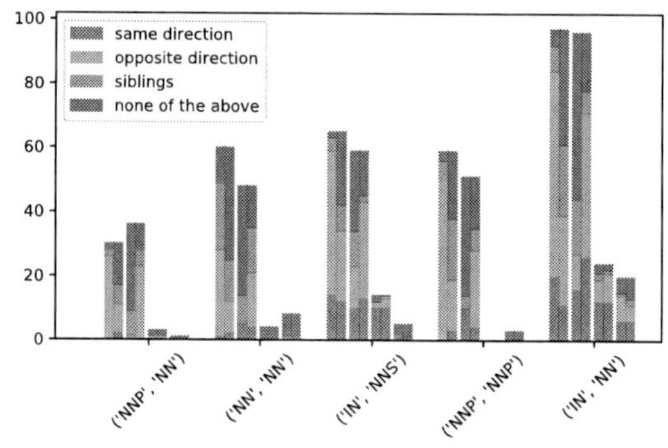


(b) DM + gold DT

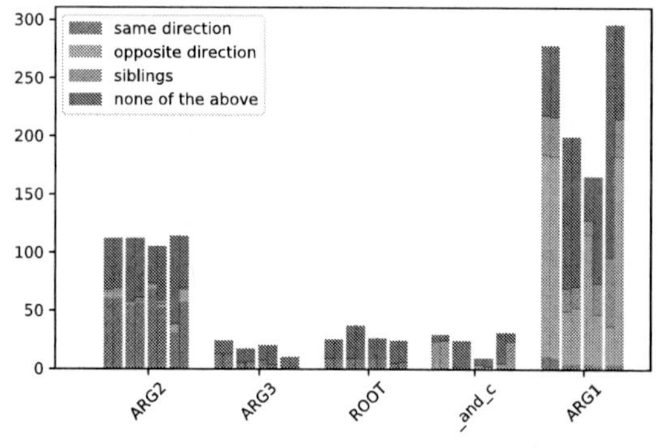


(c) DM + predicted DT

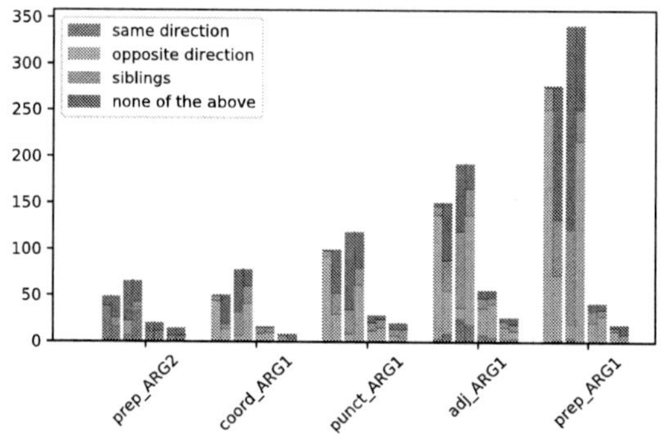


(d) PAS + gold SB

Figure 2: Error analysis for various models when informed by syntactic features, broken down by arc type and PoS pair. The four columns represent the four error types of Section 6.1 and colour distributions according to gold and predicted syntax features.

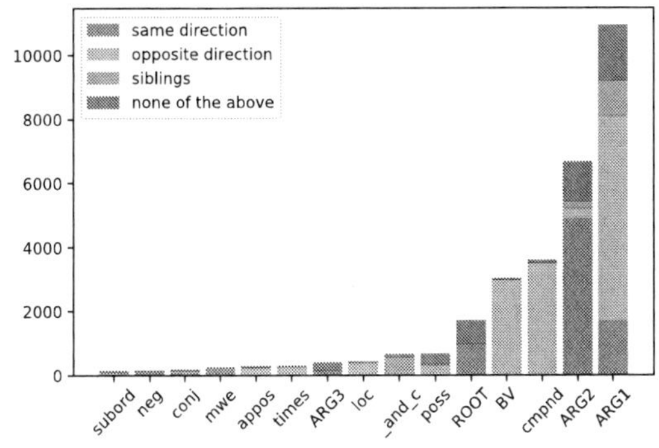


Figure 3: Relation between DM arcs and syntactic features extracted from gold-standard DT trees, broken down by arc type.

To show how syntactic heads and semantic arcs correlate independently of the parsing model, we add Figure 3. As we can see, arcs denoting the first argument of a semantic predicate (*ARG1*) occur mostly with syntactic arcs in the opposite direction. Similarly, a syntactic arc in the same direction often accompanies arcs denoting the second argument of a semantic predicate (*ARG2*); two instances from the example analysis in Figure 1 are *"take"* $\rightarrow$ *"hand"* and *"show"* $\rightarrow$ *"me"*. Another example of a clear pattern is with *compound* and conjunction (*_and_c*). Both types of arcs connect mostly nouns, but whereas *compound* arcs correlate with opposite syntactic arcs, head and dependent in a conjunction more typically share the same syntactic head (the conjunction *"and"*).

### 6.2 Results

We now explain how to read the graphs with the results of our two-dimensional error analysis for the DM parsing models. Figure 2a shows the outcome of this analysis when the model is informed by syntactic features extracted from gold-standard DT trees and evaluated on the development data. More specifically, it shows results for those five DM arc types for which adding syntax has the greatest effect on the absolute difference of mistakes relative to the baseline. For each arc type we plot four pairs of bars, one for each of the error types 1–4, from left to right. Figure 2b breaks down results by head–dependent part-of-speech pairs instead. Figure 2c compares the baseline with the model using predicted syntax, also on DM graphs and DT trees. Note that, as the ordering follows the absolute *difference* of mistakes, the arc types shown in Figure 2c are not the same as the ones in Figure 2a.

In all plots, the two bars in each of the four pairs of bars show the (colour-coded) distributions of the types (a)–(d) relative to gold-standard syntax (first bar) and predicted syntax (second bar); thus the distribution relative to the syntactic information actually used by each model is in the first bar in Figures 2a–2b (models informed by gold-standard syntax), and in the second bars in Figure 2c (models informed by predicted syntax).

### 6.3 Relation between Syntax and Semantics

To directly compare how gold-standard and predicted syntax relate to semantic arcs, we look at the differently coloured sub-columns in Figures 2a and 2b. We recall that these figures compare the no-syntax baseline to a model informed by syntactic features extracted from gold-standard analyses.

The errors avoided by the syntax-informed model (columns 1 and 2) have similar syntactic-head distributions as the general distribution in Figure 3 when looking at gold syntax. The distribution for predicted syntax does not match, due to wrong predictions when parsing these related substructures. For example, in the predicted syntax, much fewer of the avoided false negative *ARG1* arcs have syntactic arcs in the opposite direction, and instead many more of the false positives (error type 2). Using a syntactic arc in the opposite direction as an indicator, fewer false negatives would have been avoided and more false positives would have been predicted. This shows that the baseline system and the syntactic parser have difficulties analyzing the same substructures.

In Section 6 we stated that the model informed by predicted syntax increases recall at the cost of precision. This is illustrated by Figure 2c, and most pronounced for the *ARG1* type, where the number of baseline false negatives avoided by the syntax-informed model (column 1) is almost as large as the number of model false positives avoided by the baseline (column 4). The error types (a)–(d) follow the same distribution when the syntax-enhanced model improves over the baseline, but diverge when not. This finding suggests that, unsurprisingly, syntactic information helps when it is correct, and interferes otherwise. An improved system would ideally know when to trust its predicted syntax and when to rather fall back on the baseline prediction.

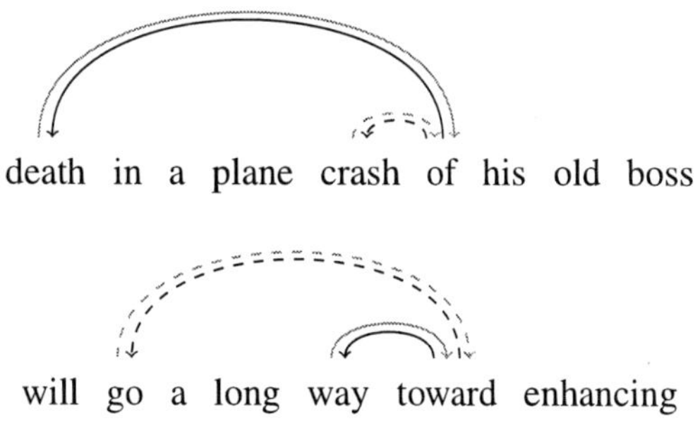


Figure 4: Graph fragments for sentences #22013118 and #22012010. Semantic arcs are shown in black, syntactic arcs in red. False negatives are drawn with continuous lines, false positives are drawn with dashed lines.

### 6.4 Where can Syntax help?

In order to better understand where syntax helps the semantic dependency parser, we look at the part-of-speech pairs of head and dependent in Figure 2b. The five pairs which receive the largest improvement when informed by gold-standard syntax can be divided into two groups:

(i) arcs between prepositions (IN) and nouns (NN, NNS)

(ii) arcs between multiple (proper) nouns (NN, NNS, NNP, NNPS)

**Prepositional Attachment** The arcs in group (i), between prepositions and nouns, represent the majority of baseline errors not only in the case of DM/DT but also in the case of PAS/SB, where they correspond (roughly) to the arc type *prep_ARG1* in Figure 2d. Figure 4 shows two graph fragments with arcs from this group; these fragments happen to be identical for DM/DT and for PAS/SB. In the two examples the gold-standard syntactic arc goes into the opposite direction than the semantic arc (our type b), and this regularity seems to be learned by the models informed by gold-standard syntax to such a degree that when the syntactic arc is incorrectly predicted, the parser also makes a corresponding mistake on the semantic side: In the examples, the prepositional phrase *"of his old boss"* is wrongly attached to the neighbouring *"plane crash"*, while *"toward"* is attached to the distant predicate *"use"* instead of the neighbouring *"way"*. Examples of this kind seem to suggest that having access to gold-standard syntax essentially 'solves' the prediction problem on the semantic side.

**Compounds and Conjuncts** The arcs in group (ii) include both compounds and conjuncts. The difficulties with compounds lie in determining which token is the governing head of the complete phrase and deciding which tokens are part of the compound. They naturally appear as part of conjunctions as well, where the difficulty of correctly identifying the heads of the two conjuncts is the same as identifying the heads of the compounds themselves. Similar to what we observed for preposition–noun arcs, having the governing head basically given by a syntactic arc, essentially eliminates the problem for compounds and conjuncts.

The example in Figure 5 showcases how failing to recognize a compound results in a cascade of follow-up mistakes. While *"guerrilla action"* is recognized as a compound, *"siege tactics"* is not. The word *"tactics"* is left out of the compound and therefore also the conjunct, receiving *"use"* as its syntactic head instead. This leads the semantic parser to not only fail to analyse the second compound and hence also the conjunct, but also attaching *"tactics"* as second argument (*ARG2*) to the predicate *"use"*, instead of the actual head of the complete phrase, *"action"*.

### 6.5 Where can Syntax not help?

While syntactic information appears to help the semantic parser in some cases, there are similar examples where syntax does not seem to be able to help at all, two of which are shown in Figure 6.

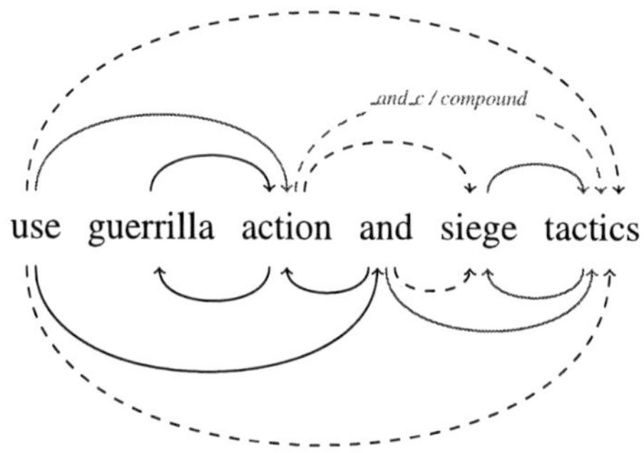


Figure 5: Graph fragments for sentence #22052046. Semantic arcs are shown above, syntactic arcs below the words. False negatives are shown in blue, false positives dashed. The blue dashed arc is an incorrectly labelled arc, annotated with the correct and the predicted label.

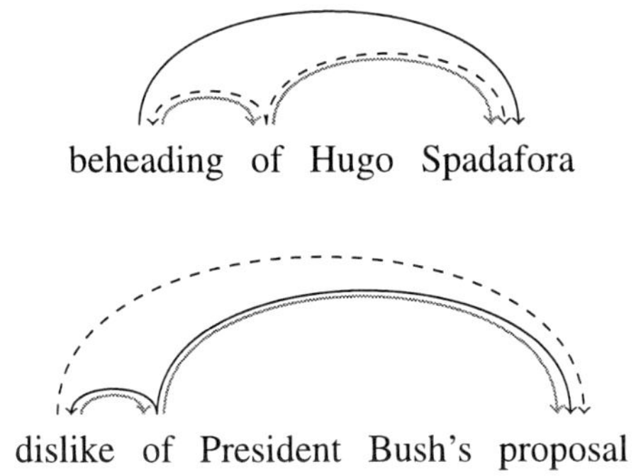


Figure 6: Graph fragments for sentences #22013141 and #22030001. Semantic arcs are shown in black, syntactic arcs in red. False negatives are drawn with continuous lines, false positives are drawn with dashed lines.

Both graph fragments contain a nominalized verb (*"beheading"* and *"dislike"*) followed by *"of"* and the object of the nominalization (*"Spadafora"* and *"proposal"*). In both cases, the parser has access to gold-standard syntax that connects the nominalization, the preposition and the object left to right. In the first instance, the parser interprets the nominalization and the object both as arguments of *"of"*, instead of directly attaching the object as an argument to the nominalization. In the second instance, the intended and observed behaviours are switched.

## 7 Conclusion

Our re-implementation of the state-of-the-art semantic dependency parsing architecture of Dozat and Manning (2018) performs on par with that system. Surprisingly, adding syntactic features to the standard lexical and morphological embeddings does not generally increase parsing accuracy. More specifically, while gold-standard syntactic information is highly beneficial, yielding accuracies significantly above the state of the art, adding predicted syntax does not lead to consistent improvements.

Our error analysis shows that there is some overlap of the information that syntactic dependency trees and semantic dependency graphs encode, in the sense that both tend to mirror each other. We have provided examples for cases that are difficult to analyze due to their inherent ambiguity. In some cases, these examples suggest that adding gold-standard syntax essentially also reveals the correct semantic analysis to the parser. This means that high-precision syntactic parsing holds significant promises even for semantic parsing, but our experiments suggest that the state of the art in syntactic dependency parsing may still be too low to fully capitalize on this potential. We believe however, that a joint syntactic–semantic parser that is able to dynamically leverage both structures (trained, perhaps, using a multi-task objective), would be an opportunity for further advances in both syntactic and semantic dependency parsing.

## Acknowledgements

We are grateful for the computational resources provided by Sigma2 in Oslo through the Nordic e-Infrastructure Collaboration (NeIC) and the Nordic Language Processing Laboratory (NLPL, `www.nlpl.eu`).

## References

Mariana S. C. Almeida and André F. T. Martins. 2015. Lisbon: Evaluating TurboSemanticParser on Multiple Languages and Out-of-Domain Data. *Proceedings of the 9th International Workshop on Semantic Evaluation (SemEval 2015)*, pages 970–973.

Junjie Cao, Sheng Huang, Weiwei Sun, and Xiaojun Wan. 2017. Parsing to 1-Endpoint-Crossing, Pagenumber-2 Graphs. *Proceedings of the 55th Annual Meeting of the Association for Computational Linguistics (Volume 1: Long Papers)*, 1:2110–2120.

Yoeng-Jin Chu and Tseng-Hong Liu. 1965. On the shortest arborescence of a directed graph. *Scientia Sinica*, 14:1396–1400.

Marie-Catherine de Marneffe and Christopher D. Manning. 2008. The Stanford Typed Dependencies Representation. In *CF+CDPE@COLING*, pages 1–8. Coling 2008 Organizing Committee.

Timothy Dozat and Christopher D. Manning. 2018. Simpler but More Accurate Semantic Dependency Parsing. *Proceedings of the 56th Annual Meeting of the Association for Computational Linguistics (Volume 2: Short Papers)*, 2:484–490.

Jack Edmonds. 1967. Optimum Branchings. *Journal of Research of the national Bureau of Standards B*, 71(4):233–240.

Dan Flickinger, Jan Hajič, Angelina Ivanova, Marco Kuhlmann, Yusuke Miyao, Stephan Oepen, and Daniel Zeman. 2016. SDP 2014 & 2015: Broad Coverage Semantic Dependency Parsing LDC2016T10.

W. Nelson Francis and Henry Kučera. 1985. Frequency Analysis of English Usage: Lexicon and Grammar. *Journal of English Linguistics*, 18(1):64–70.

Yarin Gal and Zoubin Ghahramani. 2016. A Theoretically Grounded Application of Dropout in Recurrent Neural Networks. In *Proceedings of the 30th International Conference on Neural Information Processing Systems*, NIPS'16, pages 1027–1035. Curran Associates Inc.

Jan Hajic, Eva Hajicová, Jarmila Panevová, Petr Sgall, Ondřej Bojar, Silvie Cinková, Eva Fučiková, Marie Mikulová, Petr Pajas, Jan Popelka, Jiří Semecký, Jana Sindlerová, Jan Sťepánek, Josef Toman, Zdenka Uresová, and Zdenek Zabokrtský. 2012. Announcing Prague Czech-English Dependency Treebank 2.0. In *Proceedings of the 8th International Conference on Language Resources and Evaluation (LREC 2012)*, pages 3153–3160, İstanbul, Turkey. European Language Resources Association.

Sepp Hochreiter and Jürgen Schmidhuber. 1997. Long Short-term Memory. *Neural computation*, 9:1735–80.

Angelina Ivanova, Stephan Oepen, Lilja Øvrelid, and Dan Flickinger. 2012. Who Did What to Whom?: A Contrastive Study of Syntacto-semantic Dependencies. In *Proceedings of the Sixth Linguistic Annotation Workshop*, LAW VI '12, pages 2–11, Stroudsburg, PA, USA. Association for Computational Linguistics.

Diederik P. Kingma and Jimmy Ba. 2014. Adam: A Method for Stochastic Optimization. *CoRR*, abs/1412.6980.

Marco Kuhlmann and Peter Jonsson. 2015. Parsing to Noncrossing Dependency Graphs. *Transactions of the Association of Computational Linguistics*, 3(1):559–570.

Mitchell P. Marcus, Mary Ann Marcinkiewicz, and Beatrice Santorini. 1993. Building a Large Annotated Corpus of English: The Penn Treebank. *Comput. Linguist.*, 19(2):313–330.

Stephen Merity, Nitish Shirish Keskar, and Richard Socher. 2017. Regularizing and Optimizing LSTM Language Models. *CoRR*, abs/1708.02182.

Yusuke Miyao. 2006. *From Linguistic Theory to Syntactic Analysis: Corpus-Oriented Grammar Development and Feature Forest Model.* Ph.D. thesis.

Joakim Nivre, Željko Agić, Lars Ahrenberg, Maria Jesus Aranzabe, Masayuki Asahara, Aitziber Atutxa, Miguel Ballesteros, John Bauer, Kepa Bengoetxea, Riyaz Ahmad Bhat, Eckhard Bick, Cristina Bosco, Gosse Bouma, Sam Bowman, Marie Candito, Gülşen Cebiroğlu Eryiğit, Giuseppe G. A. Celano, Fabricio Chalub, Jinho Choi, Çağrı Çöltekin, Miriam Connor, Elizabeth Davidson, Marie-Catherine de Marneffe, Valeria de Paiva, Arantza Diaz de Ilarraza, Kaja Dobrovoljc, Timothy Dozat, Kira Droganova, Puneet Dwivedi, Marhaba Eli, Tomaž Erjavec, Richárd Farkas, Jennifer Foster, Cláudia Freitas, Katarína Gajdošová, Daniel Galbraith, Marcos Garcia, Filip Ginter, Iakes Goenaga, Koldo Gojenola, Memduh Gökırmak, Yoav Goldberg, Xavier Gómez Guinovart, Berta Gonzáles Saavedra, Matias Grioni, Normunds Grūzītis, Bruno Guillaume, Nizar Habash, Jan Hajič, Linh Hà Mỹ, Dag Haug, Barbora Hladká, Petter Hohle, Radu Ion, Elena Irimia, Anders Johannsen, Fredrik Jørgensen, Hüner Kaşıkara, Hiroshi Kanayama, Jenna Kanerva, Natalia Kotsyba, Simon Krek, Veronika Laippala, Phuong Lê H`ông, Alessandro Lenci, Nikola Ljubešić, Olga Lyashevskaya, Teresa Lynn, Aibek Makazhanov, Christopher Manning, Cătălina Mărănduc, David Mareček, Héctor Martínez Alonso, André Martins, Jan Mašek, Yuji Matsumoto, Ryan McDonald, Anna Missilä, Verginica Mititelu, Yusuke Miyao, Simonetta Montemagni, Amir More, Shunsuke Mori, Bohdan Moskalevskyi, Kadri Muischnek, Nina Mustafina, Kaili Müürisep, Luong Nguyễn Th i, Huyền Nguyễn Th i Minh, Vitaly Nikolaev, Hanna Nurmi, Stina Ojala, Petya Osenova, Lilja Øvrelid, Elena Pascual, Marco Passarotti, Cenel-Augusto Perez, Guy Perrier, Slav Petrov, Jussi Piitulainen, Barbara Plank, Martin Popel, Lauma Pretkalniņa, Prokopis Prokopidis, Tiina Puolakainen, Sampo Pyysalo, Alexandre Rademaker, Loganathan Ramasamy, Livy Real, Laura Rituma, Rudolf Rosa, Shadi Saleh, Manuela Sanguinetti, Baiba Saulīte, Sebastian Schuster, Djamé Seddah, Wolfgang Seeker, Mojgan Seraji, Lena Shakurova, Mo Shen, Dmitry Sichinava, Natalia Silveira, Maria Simi, Radu Simionescu, Katalin Simkó, Mária Šimková, Kiril Simov, Aaron Smith, Alane Suhr, Umut Sulubacak, Zsolt Szántó, Dima Taji, Takaaki Tanaka, Reut Tsarfaty, Francis Tyers, Sumire Uematsu, Larraitz Uria, Gertjan van Noord, Viktor Varga, Veronika Vincze, Jonathan North Washington, Zdeněk Žabokrtský, Amir Zeldes, Daniel Zeman, and Hanzhi Zhu. 2017. Universal Dependencies 2.0.

Stephan Oepen, Marco Kuhlmann, Yusuke Miyao, Daniel Zeman, Silvie Cinkova, Dan Flickinger, Jan Hajic, and Zdenka Uresova. 2015. SemEval 2015 Task 18: Broad-Coverage Semantic Dependency Parsing. *Proceedings of the 9th International Workshop on Semantic Evaluation (SemEval 2015)*, pages 915–926.

Stephan Oepen, Marco Kuhlmann, Yusuke Miyao, Daniel Zeman, Dan Flickinger, Jan Hajic, Angelina Ivanova, and Yi Zhang. 2014. SemEval 2014 Task 8: Broad-Coverage Semantic Dependency Parsing. *Proceedings of the 8th International Workshop on Semantic Evaluation (SemEval 2014)*, pages 63–72.

Stephan Oepen and Jan Tore Lønning. 2006. Discriminant-Based MRS Banking. In *Proceedings of the Fifth International Conference on Language Resources and Evaluation (LREC-2006)*, Genoa, Italy. European Language Resources Association (ELRA).

Hao Peng, Sam Thomson, and Noah A. Smith. 2017. Deep Multitask Learning for Semantic Dependency

Parsing. *Proceedings of the 55th Annual Meeting of the Association for Computational Linguistics (Volume 1: Long Papers)*, 1:2037–2048.

Hao Peng, Sam Thomson, and Noah A. Smith. 2018. Backpropagating through Structured Argmax using a SPIGOT. In *Proceedings of the 56th Annual Meeting of the Association for Computational Linguistics (Volume 1: Long Papers)*, pages 1863–1873, Melbourne, Australia. Association for Computational Linguistics.

Jeffrey Pennington, Richard Socher, and Christopher D. Manning. 2014. GloVe: Global Vectors for Word Representation. In *Empirical Methods in Natural Language Processing (EMNLP)*, pages 1532–1543.

Peng Qi, Timothy Dozat, Yuhao Zhang, and Christopher D. Manning. 2018. Universal Dependency Parsing from Scratch. In *Proceedings of the CoNLL 2018 Shared Task: Multilingual Parsing from Raw Text to Universal Dependencies*, pages 160–170. Association for Computational Linguistics.

Daniel Roxbo. 2019. A Detailed Analysis of Semantic Dependency Parsing with Deep Neural Networks. Master's thesis, Linköping University, Human-Centered systems.

Milan Straka and Jana Straková. 2017. Tokenizing, POS Tagging, Lemmatizing and Parsing UD 2.0 with UDPipe. In *Proceedings of the CoNLL 2017 Shared Task: Multilingual Parsing from Raw Text to Universal Dependencies*, pages 88–99. Association for Computational Linguistics.

Daniel Varab and Natalie Schluter. 2018. UniParse: A universal graph-based parsing toolkit. *CoRR*, abs/1807.04053.

Li Wan, Matthew Zeiler, Sixin Zhang, Yann LeCun, and Rob Fergus. 2013. Regularization of Neural Networks Using Dropconnect. In *Proceedings of the 30th International Conference on International Conference on Machine Learning - Volume 28*, ICML'13, pages III–1058–III–1066. JMLR.org.

Yuxuan Wang, Wanxiang Che, Jiang Guo, and Ting Liu. 2018. A Neural Transition-Based Approach for Semantic Dependency Graph Parsing. In *AAAI*, pages 5561–5568. AAAI Press.

Xun Zhang, Yantao Du, Weiwei Sun, and Xiaojun Wan. 2016. Transition-Based Parsing for Deep Dependency Structures. *Computational Linguistics*, 42(3):353–389.

# To Lemmatize or Not to Lemmatize: How Word Normalisation Affects ELMo Performance in Word Sense Disambiguation

**Andrey Kutuzov***
University of Oslo
Oslo, Norway
andreku@ifi.uio.no

**Elizaveta Kuzmenko**
University of Trento
Trento, Italy
lizaku77@gmail.com

## Abstract

In this paper, we critically evaluate the widespread assumption that deep learning NLP models do not require lemmatized input. To test this, we trained versions of contextualised word embedding *ELMo* models on raw tokenized corpora and on the corpora with word tokens replaced by their lemmas. Then, these models were evaluated on the word sense disambiguation task. This was done for the English and Russian languages.

The experiments showed that while lemmatization is indeed not necessary for English, the situation is different for Russian. It seems that for rich-morphology languages, using lemmatized training and testing data yields small but consistent improvements: at least for word sense disambiguation. This means that the decisions about text pre-processing before training *ELMo* should consider the linguistic nature of the language in question.

## 1 Introduction

Deep contextualised representations of linguistic entities (words and/or sentences) are used in many current state-of-the-art NLP systems. The most well-known examples of such models are arguably *ELMo* (Peters et al., 2018) and *BERT* (Devlin et al., 2019).

A long-standing tradition if the field of applying deep learning to NLP tasks can be summarised as follows: as minimal pre-processing as possible. It is widely believed that lemmatization or other text input normalisation is not necessary. Advanced neural architectures based on character input (CNNs, BPE, etc) are supposed to be able to learn how to handle spelling and morphology variations themselves, even for languages with rich morphology: 'just add more layers!'. Contextualised embedding models follow this tradition: as a rule, they are trained on raw text collections, with minimal linguistic pre-processing. Below, we show that this is not entirely true.

It is known that for the previous generation of word embedding models ('static' ones like *word2vec* (Mikolov et al., 2013), where a word always has the same representation regardless of the context in which it occurs), lemmatization of the training and testing data improves their performance. Fares et al. (2017) showed that this is true at least for semantic similarity and analogy tasks.

In this paper, we describe our experiments in finding out whether lemmatization helps modern contextualised embeddings (on the example of *ELMo*). We compare the performance of *ELMo* models trained on the same corpus before and after lemmatization. It is impossible to evaluate contextualised models on 'static' tasks like lexical semantic similarity or word analogies. Because of this, we turned to **word sense disambiguation in context** (WSD) as an evaluation task.

In brief, we use contextualised representations of ambiguous words from the top layer of an *ELMo* model to train word sense classifiers and find out whether using lemmas instead of tokens helps in this task (see Section 5). We experiment with the English and Russian languages and show that they differ significantly in the influence of lemmatization on the WSD performance of ELMo models.

Our findings and the contributions of this paper are:

1. Linguistic text pre-processing still matters in some tasks, even for contemporary deep representation learning algorithms.

2. For the Russian language, with its rich mor-

*Both authors contributed equally to the paper.

|  | English | Russian |
|---|---|---|
| **Source** | Wikipedia | Wikipedia + RNC |
| **Size, tokens** | 2 174 mln | 989 mln |
| **Size, lemmas** | 1 977 mln | 988 mln |

Table 1: Training corpora

phology, lemmatizing the training and testing data for *ELMo* representations yields small but consistent improvements in the WSD task. This is unlike English, where the differences are negligible.

## 2 Related work

*ELMo* contextual word representations are learned in an unsupervised way through language modelling (Peters et al., 2018). The general architecture consists of a two-layer BiLSTM on top of a convolutional layer which takes character sequences as its input. Since the model uses fully character-based token representations, it avoids the problem of out-of-vocabulary words. Because of this, the authors explicitly recommend not to use any normalisation except tokenization for the input text. However, as we show below, while this is true for English, for other languages feeding *ELMo* with lemmas instead of raw tokens can improve WSD performance.

Word sense disambiguation or WSD (Navigli, 2009) is the NLP task consisting of choosing a word sense from a pre-defined sense inventory, given the context in which the word is used. WSD fits well into our aim to intrinsically evaluate *ELMo* models, since solving the problem of polysemy and homonymy was one of the original promises of contextualised embeddings: their primary difference from the previous generation of word embedding models is that contextualised approaches generate different representations for homographs depending on the context. We use two lexical sample WSD test sets, further described in Section 4.

## 3 Training ELMo

For the experiments described below, we trained our own *ELMo* models from scratch. For English, the training corpus consisted of the English Wikipedia dump[1] from February 2017. For Russian, it was a concatenation of the Russian Wikipedia dump from December 2018 and the full Russian National Corpus[2] (RNC). The RNC texts were added to the Russian Wikipedia dump so as to make the Russian training corpus more comparable in size to the English one (Wikipedia texts would comprise only half of the size). As Table 1 shows, the English Wikipedia is still two times larger, but at least the order is the same.

The texts were tokenized and lemmatized with the *UDPipe* models for the respective languages trained on the Universal Dependencies 2.3 treebanks (Straka and Straková, 2017). *UDPipe* yields lemmatization accuracy about 96% for English and 97% for Russian[3]; thus for the task at hand, we considered it to be gold and did not try to further improve the quality of normalisation itself (although it is not entirely error-free, see Section 4).

*ELMo* models were trained on these corpora using the original TensorFlow implementation[4], for 3 epochs with batch size 192, on two GPUs. To train faster, we decreased the dimensionality of the LSTM layers from the default 4096 to 2048 for all the models.

## 4 Word sense disambiguation test sets

We used two WSD datasets for evaluation:

- *Senseval-3* for English (Mihalcea et al., 2004)
- *RUSSE'18* for Russian (Panchenko et al., 2018)

The *Senseval-3* dataset consists of lexical samples for nouns, verbs and adjectives; we used only noun target words:

1. *argument*
2. *arm*
3. *atmosphere*
4. *audience*
5. *bank*
6. *degree*
7. *difference*
8. *difficulty*

[1] https://dumps.wikimedia.org/

[2] http://ruscorpora.ru/en/

[3] http://ufal.mff.cuni.cz/udpipe/models#universal_dependencies_23_models

[4] https://github.com/allenai/bilm-tf

9. *disc*
10. *image*
11. *interest*
12. *judgement*
13. *organization*
14. *paper*
15. *party*
16. *performance*
17. *plan*
18. *shelter*
19. *sort*
20. *source*

An example for the ambiguous word *argument* is given below:

*In some situations Postscript can be faster than the escape sequence type of printer control file. It uses post fix notation, where* ***arguments*** *come first and operators follow. This is basically the same as Reverse Polish Notation as used on certain calculators, and follows directly from the stack based approach.*

It this sentence, the word '*argument*' is used in the sense of a mathematical operator.

The *RUSSE'18* dataset was created in 2018 for the shared task in Russian word sense induction. This dataset contains only nouns; the list of words with their English translations is given in Table 2.

Originally, it includes also the words байка 'tale/fleece' and гвоздика 'clove/small nail', but their senses are ambiguous only in some inflectional forms (not in lemmas), therefore we decided to exclude these words from evaluation.

The Russian dataset is more homogeneous compared to the English one, as for all the target words there is approximately the same number of context words in the examples. This is achieved by applying the lexical window (25 words before and after the target word) and cropping everything that falls outside of that window. In the English dataset, on the contrary, the whole paragraph with the target word is taken into account. We have tried cropping the examples for English as well, but it did not result in any change in the quality of classification. In the end, we decided not to apply the lexical window to the English dataset so as not to alter it and rather use it in the original form.

| Target word | Translation |
|---|---|
| акция | 'stock/marketing event' |
| гипербола | 'hyperbola/exaggeration' |
| град | 'hail/city' |
| гусеница | 'caterpillar/track' |
| домино | 'dominoes/costume' |
| кабачок | 'squash/restaurant' |
| капот | 'hood (part of a car/clothing)' |
| карьер | 'mine/fast pace of a horse' |
| кок | 'cook/hairstyle' |
| крона | 'crown (tree/coin)' |
| круп | 'crupper (part of a horse/illness)' |
| мандарин | 'fruit/a Chinese official' |
| рок | 'rock (music/destiny)' |
| слог | 'syllable/text style' |
| стопка | 'stack/glass' |
| таз | 'basin/human body part' |
| такса | 'tariff/dog breed' |
| шах | 'check/prince' |

Table 2: Target ambiguous words for Russian (*RUSSE'18*)

Here is an example from the *RUSSE'18* for the ambiguous word мандарин 'mandarin' in the sense 'Chinese official title':

"...дипломатического корпуса останкам богдыхана и императрицы обставлено было с необычайной торжественностью. Тысячи мандаринов и других высокопоставленных лиц разместились шпалерами на трех мраморных террасах ведущих к..."

'...the diplomatic bodies of the Bogdikhan and the Empress was furnished with extraordinary solemnity. Thousands of mandarins and other dignitaries were placed on three marble terraces leading to...'.

Table 3 compares both datasets. Before usage, they were pre-processed in the same way as the training corpora for *ELMo* (see Section 3), thus producing a lemmatized and a non-lemmatized versions of each.

As we can see from Table 3, for 20 target words in English there are 24 lemmas, and for 18 target words in Russian there are 36 different lemmas. These numbers are explained by occasional errors in the *UDPipe* lemmatization. Another interesting thing to observe is the number of distinct

| Property | Senseval-3 | RUSSE'18 |
|---|---|---|
| **Target words** | 20 | 18 |
| **Distinct target forms** | 39 | 132 |
| **Distinct target lemmas** | 24 | 36 |
| **Examples per target** | 171 | 126 |
| **Tokens per example** | 126 | 25 |
| **Senses per target** | 6 | 2 |

Table 3: Characteristics of the WSD datasets. The numbers in the lower part are average values.

word forms for every language. For English, there are 39 distinct forms for 20 target nouns: singular and plural for every noun, except '*atmosphere*' which is used only in the singular form. Thus, inflectional variability of English nouns is covered by the dataset almost completely. For Russian, we observe 132 distinct forms for 18 target nouns, giving more than 7 inflectional forms per each word. Note that this still covers only half of all the inflectional variability of Russian: this language features 12 distinct forms for each noun (6 cases and 2 numbers).

To sum up, the *RUSSE'18* dataset is morphologically far more complex than the *Senseval3*, reflecting the properties of the respective languages. In the next section we will see that this leads to substantial differences regarding comparisons between token-based and lemma-based *ELMo* models.

## 5 Experiments

Following Gorman and Bedrick (2019), we decided to avoid using any standard train-test splits for our WSD datasets. Instead, we rely on per-word random splits and 5-fold cross-validation. This means that for each target word we randomly generate 5 different divisions of its context sentences list into train and test sets, and then train and test 5 different classifier models on this data. The resulting performance score for each target word is the average of 5 macro-F1 scores produced by these classifiers.

*ELMo* models can be employed for the WSD task in two different ways: either by fine-tuning the model or by extracting word representations from it and then using them as features in a downstream classifier. We decided to stick to the second (feature extraction) approach, since it is conceptually and computationally simpler. Additionally, Peters et al. (2019) showed that for most NLP tasks (except those focused on sentence pairs) the performance of feature extraction and fine-tuning is nearly the same. Thus we extracted the single vector of the target word from the *ELMo* top layer ('target' rows in Table 4) or the averaged *ELMo* top layer vectors of all words in the context sentence ('averaged' rows in Table 4).

| Model | English | Russian |
|---|---|---|
| | Baselines | |
| Random | $\approx 0.138$ | $\approx 0.444$ |
| MFS | 0.119 | 0.391 |
| | Tokens | |
| SGNS (averaged) | 0.299 | 0.851 |
| *ELMo* (averaged) | 0.362 | 0.885 |
| *ELMo* (target) | 0.463 | 0.875 |
| | Lemmas | |
| SGNS (averaged) | 0.300 | 0.854 |
| *ELMo* (averaged) | 0.365 | 0.888 |
| *ELMo* (target) | 0.452 | **0.907** |

Table 4: Averaged macro-F1 scores for WSD

For comparison, we also report the scores of the 'averaged vectors' representations with Continuous Skipgram (Mikolov et al., 2013) embedding models trained on the English or Russian Wikipedia dumps ('SGNS' rows): before the advent of contextualised models, this was one of the most widely used ways to 'squeeze' the meaning of a sentence into a fixed-size vector. Of course it does not mean that the meaning of a sentence always determines the senses all its words are used in. However, averaging representations of words in contexts as a proxy to the sense of one particular word is a long established tradition in WSD, starting at least from Schütze (1998). Also, since SGNS is a 'static' embedding model, it is of course not possible to use only target word vectors as features: they would be identical whatever the context is.

Simple logistic regression was used as a classification algorithm. We also tested a multi-layer perceptron (MLP) classifier with 200-neurons hidden layer, which yielded essentially the same results. This leads us to believe that our findings are not classifier-dependent.

Table 4 shows the results, together with the ran-

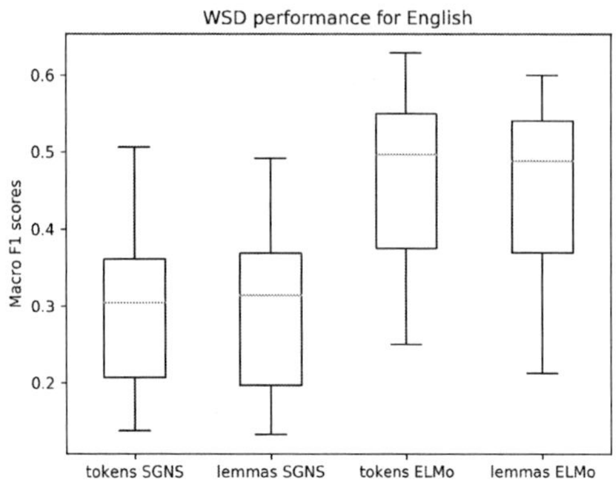


Figure 1: Word sense disambiguation performance on the **English** data across words (*ELMo* target models).

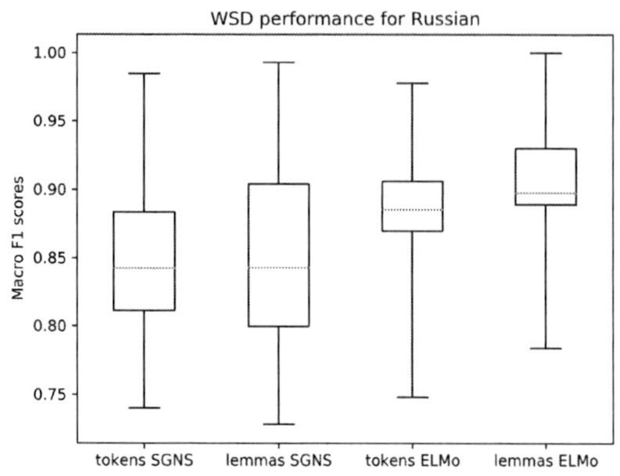


Figure 2: Word sense disambiguation performance on the **Russian** data across words (*ELMo* target models).

dom and most frequent sense (MFS) baselines for each dataset.

First, *ELMo* outperforms SGNS for both languages, which comes as no surprise. Second, the approach with averaging representations from all words in the sentence is not beneficial for WSD with *ELMo*: for English data, it clearly loses to a single target word representation, and for Russian there are no significant differences (and using a single target word is preferable from the computational point of view, since it does not require the averaging operation). Thus, below we discuss only the single target word usage mode of *ELMo*.

But the most important part is the comparison between using tokens or lemmas in the train and test data. For the 'static' SGNS embeddings, it does not significantly change the WSD scores for both languages. The same is true for English *ELMo* models, where differences are negligible and seem to be simple fluctuations. However, for Russian, *ELMo* (target) on lemmas outperforms *ELMo* on tokens, with small but significant[5] improvement. The most plausible explanation for this is that (despite of purely character-based input of *ELMo*) the model does not have to learn idiosyncrasies of a particular language morphology. Instead, it can use its (limited) capacity to better learn lexical semantic structures, leading to better WSD performance. The box plots 1 and 2 illustrate the scores dispersion across words in the test sets for English and Russian correspondingly (orange lines are medians). In the next section 6 we analyse the results qualitatively.

[5] At $p$ value of 0.1, according to the Welch's t-test.

| Word | Tokens | Lemmas | STD |
|---|---|---|---|
| акция | 0.876 | **0.978** | 0.050 |
| крона | 0.978 | **1.000** | 0.018 |
| круп | 0.927 | **1.000** | 0.070 |
| домино | **0.910** | 0.874 | 0.057 |

Table 5: F1 scores for target words from *RUSSE'18* with significant differences between lemma-based and token-based models

## 6 Qualitative analysis

In this section we focus on the comparison of scores for the Russian dataset. The classifier for Russian had to choose between fewer classes (two or three), which made the scores higher and more consistent than for the English dataset. Overall, we see improvements in the scores for the majority of words, which proves that lemmatization for morphologically rich languages is beneficial.

We decided to analyse more closely those words for which the difference in the scores between lemma-based and token-based models was statistically significant. By 'significant' we mean that the scores differ by more that one standard deviation (the largest standard deviation value in the two sets was taken). The resulting list of targets words with significant difference in scores is given in Table 5.

We can see that among 18 words in the dataset only 3 exhibit significant improvement in their scores when moving from tokens to lemmas in the input data. It shows that even though the overall F1 scores for the Russian data have shown the plausibility of lemmatization, this improvement is mostly driven by a few words. It should be noted that these words' scores feature very low standard deviation values (for other words, standard deviation values were above 0.1, making F1 differences insignificant). Such a behaviour can be caused by more consistent differentiation of context for various senses of these 3 words. For example, with the word кабачок 'squash / small restaurant', the contexts for both senses can be similar, since they are all related to food. This makes the WSD scores unstable. On the other hand, for акция 'stock, share / event', крона 'crown (tree / coin)' or круп 'croup (horse body part / illness)', their senses are not related, which resulted in more stable results and significant difference in the scores (see Table 5).

There is only one word in the RUSSE'18 dataset for which the score has strongly decreased when moving to lemma-based models: домино 'domino (game / costume)'. In fact, the score difference here lies on the border of one standard deviation, so strictly speaking it is not really significant. However, the word still presents an interesting phenomenon.

Домино is the only target noun in the RUSSE'18 that has no inflected forms, since it is a borrowed word. This leaves no room for improvement when using lemma-based *ELMo* models: all tokens of this word are already identical. At the same time, some information about inflected word forms in the context can be useful, but it is lost during lemmatization, and this leads to the decreased score. Arguably, this means that lemmatization brings along both advantages and disadvantages for WSD with *ELMo*. For inflected words (which constitute the majority of Russian vocabulary) profits outweigh the losses, but for atypical non-changeable words it can be the opposite.

The scores for the excluded target words байка 'tale / fleece' and гвоздика 'clove / small nail' are given in Table 6 (recall that they were excluded because of being ambiguous only in some inflectional forms). For these words we can see a great improvement with lemma-based models. This, of course stems from the fact that these words in different senses have different lemmas. Therefore, the results are heavily dependent on the quality of lemmatization.

| Word | Tokens | Lemmas | STD |
|---|---|---|---|
| байка | 0.421 | **0.627** | 0.099 |
| гвоздика | 0.553 | **0.619** | 0.038 |

Table 6: F1 scores for the excluded target words from *RUSSE'18*.

## 7 Conclusion

We evaluated how the ability of *ELMo* contextualised word embedding models to disambiguate word senses depends on the nature of the training data. In particular, we compared the models trained on raw tokenized corpora and those trained on the corpora with word tokens replaced by their normal forms (lemmas). The models we trained are publicly available via the NLPL word embeddings repository[6] (Fares et al., 2017).

In the majority of research papers on deep learning approaches to NLP, it is assumed that lemmatization is not necessary, especially when using powerful contextualised embeddings. Our experiments show that this is indeed true for languages with simple morphology (like English). However, for rich-morphology languages (like Russian), using lemmatized training data yields small but consistent improvements in the word sense disambiguation task. These improvements are not observed for rare words which lack inflected forms; this further supports our hypothesis that better WSD scores of lemma-based models are related to them better handling multiple word forms in morphology-rich languages.

Of course, lemmatization is by all means not a silver bullet. In other tasks, where inflectional properties of words are important, it can even hurt the performance. But this is true for any NLP systems, not only deep learning based ones.

The take-home message here is twofold: first, text pre-processing still matters for contemporary deep learning algorithms. Their impressive learning abilities do not always allow them to infer normalisation rules themselves, from simply optimising the language modelling task. Second, the nature of language at hand matters as well, and differences in this nature can result in different decisions being optimal or sub-optimal at the stage of deep learning models training. The simple truth 'English is not representative of all languages on Earth' still holds here.

[6] http://vectors.nlpl.eu/repository/

In the future, we plan to extend our work by including more languages into the analysis. Using Russian and English allowed us to hypothesise about the importance of morphological character of a language. But we only scratched the surface of the linguistic diversity. To verify this claim, it is necessary to analyse more strongly inflected languages like Russian as well as more weakly inflected (analytical) languages similar to English. This will help to find out if the inflection differences are important for training deep learning models across human languages in general.

## References


Jacob Devlin, Ming-Wei Chang, Kenton Lee, and Kristina Toutanova. 2019. BERT: Pre-training of deep bidirectional transformers for language understanding. In *Proceedings of the 2019 Conference of the North American Chapter of the Association for Computational Linguistics: Human Language Technologies, Volume 1 (Long and Short Papers)*, pages 4171–4186, Minneapolis, Minnesota. Association for Computational Linguistics.

Murhaf Fares, Andrey Kutuzov, Stephan Oepen, and Erik Velldal. 2017. Word vectors, reuse, and replicability: Towards a community repository of large-text resources. In *Proceedings of the 21st Nordic Conference on Computational Linguistics*, pages 271–276, Gothenburg, Sweden. Association for Computational Linguistics.

Kyle Gorman and Steven Bedrick. 2019. We need to talk about standard splits. In *Proceedings of the 57th Annual Meeting of the Association for Computational Linguistics*, pages 2786–2791, Florence, Italy. Association for Computational Linguistics.

Rada Mihalcea, Timothy Chklovski, and Adam Kilgarriff. 2004. The Senseval-3 English lexical sample task. In *Proceedings of SENSEVAL-3, the Third International Workshop on the Evaluation of Systems for the Semantic Analysis of Text*, pages 25–28, Barcelona, Spain. Association for Computational Linguistics.

Tomas Mikolov, Ilya Sutskever, Kai Chen, Greg S Corrado, and Jeff Dean. 2013. Distributed representations of words and phrases and their compositionality. *Advances in Neural Information Processing Systems 26*, pages 3111–3119.

Roberto Navigli. 2009. Word sense disambiguation: A survey. *ACM computing surveys (CSUR)*, 41(2):10.

Alexander Panchenko, Anastasia Lopukhina, Dmitry Ustalov, Konstantin Lopukhin, Nikolay Arefyev, Alexey Leontyev, and Natalia Loukachevitch. 2018. RUSSE'2018: A Shared Task on Word Sense Induction for the Russian Language. In *Computational Linguistics and Intellectual Technologies: Papers from the Annual International Conference "Dialogue"*, pages 547–564, Moscow, Russia. RSUH.

Matthew Peters, Mark Neumann, Mohit Iyyer, Matt Gardner, Christopher Clark, Kenton Lee, and Luke Zettlemoyer. 2018. Deep contextualized word representations. In *Proceedings of the 2018 Conference of the North American Chapter of the Association for Computational Linguistics: Human Language Technologies, Volume 1 (Long Papers)*, pages 2227–2237, New Orleans, Louisiana. Association for Computational Linguistics.

Matthew E. Peters, Sebastian Ruder, and Noah A. Smith. 2019. To tune or not to tune? Adapting pretrained representations to diverse tasks. In *Proceedings of the 4th Workshop on Representation Learning for NLP (RepL4NLP-2019)*, pages 7–14, Florence, Italy. Association for Computational Linguistics.

Hinrich Schütze. 1998. Automatic word sense discrimination. *Computational Linguistics*, 24(1):97–123.

Milan Straka and Jana Straková. 2017. Tokenizing, POS tagging, lemmatizing and parsing UD 2.0 with UDPipe. In *Proceedings of the CoNLL 2017 Shared Task: Multilingual Parsing from Raw Text to Universal Dependencies*, pages 88–99, Vancouver, Canada. Association for Computational Linguistics.

# Is Multilingual BERT Fluent in Language Generation?

**Samuel Rönnqvist*** **Jenna Kanerva*** **Tapio Salakoski** **Filip Ginter***
TurkuNLP
Department of Future Technologies
University of Turku, Finland
{saanro, jmnybl, sala, figint}@utu.fi

## Abstract

The multilingual BERT model is trained on 104 languages and meant to serve as a universal language model and tool for encoding sentences. We explore how well the model performs on several languages across several tasks: a diagnostic classification probing the embeddings for a particular syntactic property, a cloze task testing the language modelling ability to fill in gaps in a sentence, and a natural language generation task testing for the ability to produce coherent text fitting a given context. We find that the currently available multilingual BERT model is clearly inferior to the monolingual counterparts, and cannot in many cases serve as a substitute for a well-trained monolingual model. We find that the English and German models perform well at generation, whereas the multilingual model is lacking, in particular, for Nordic languages.[1]

## 1 Introduction

The language representation model BERT (Bidirectional Encoder Representations from Transformers) has been shown to achieve state-of-the-art performance when fine-tuned on a range of downstream tasks related to language understanding (Devlin et al., 2018), and recently also language generation. In addition to downstream applications, many recent studies have explored more directly how various types of linguistic information is captured in BERT's representations.

However, all such studies we are aware of are conducted for English using the monolingual BERT model as the availability of pre-trained BERT models for other languages is extremely scarce. For the vast majority of languages, the only option is the multilingual BERT model trained jointly on 104 languages. In "coffee break" discussions, it is often mentioned that the multilingual BERT model lags behind the monolingual models in terms of quality and cannot serve as a drop-in replacement.

In this paper, we therefore set out to test the multilingual model on several tasks and several languages (primarily Nordic), to establish whether, and to what extent this is the case, as well as to establish at least an order-of-magnitude expectation of the performance of the present multilingual BERT model on these tasks and languages. It must be stressed that this paper deals with the particular multilingual model distributed by the BERT creators, rather than the more general question of comparison of the multilingual and monolingual training schedule. Studying those questions would necessitate training multilingual BERT models with resource requirements far beyond those at our disposal.

We put a particular focus on the natural language generation (NLG) task, which we hypothesize requires a deeper understanding of the language in question on the side of the model. We take English and German, for which monolingual versions of BERT are available, as reference languages, in order to compare how they perform in the mono- vs. multilingual settings. Furthermore, we perform experiments with the Nordic languages of Danish, Finnish, Norwegian (Bokmål and Nynorsk) and Swedish, with in-depth evaluations on Finnish and Swedish, as well as the abovementioned two reference languages.

## 2 Related Work

A BERT model is comprised of several layers of stacked Transformer networks (Vaswani et al.,

*The marked authors contributed equally to this paper.

[1]The code of the experiments in the paper is available at: https://github.com/TurkuNLP/bert-eval

2017), each providing representations of both the input sequence and its individual tokens. The model incorporates a tokenizer that splits an input sentence into words, or subword units for words or word forms that are relatively infrequent in the training data.

Several recent studies have explored how BERT captures linguistic information in English, and how it is distributed across layers. (Tenney et al., 2019; Jawahar et al., 2019; Clark et al., 2019) A particular line of inquiry has focused on how much hierarchical understanding of a language and knowledge of the syntactic structure is captured in the word representations of the monolingual English BERT model. In Goldberg (2019), the BERT models are shown to perform well on capturing several syntactic phenomena of the English language. The paper shows the model to favor the correct subject-verb agreement over the wrong one even if the input is crafted to mislead the model with agreement attractors, i.e. an intervening subordinate clause with opposite number of the subject. BERT is also shown to perform well on the agreement task even if tokens are randomly substituted from the same part-of-speech category, making the input semantically meaningless while preserving the syntactic structure.

Similarly, Ettinger (2019) evaluates the BERT model on several English psycholinguistic datasets, where the model is shown generally being able to distinguish a good completion from a bad one, while still failing in some more complex categories, for example being insensitive to negation.

Lin et al. (2019) uses a diagnostic classifier to study to which extent syntactic or positional information can be predicted from the English BERT embeddings, and how this information is carried through the different layers.

The multilingual BERT model is studied in the context of zero-shot cross-lingual transfer, where it is shown to perform competitively to other transfer models. (Pires et al., 2019; Wu and Dredze, 2019)

Text generation with BERT is introduced by Wang and Cho (2019), who demonstrate several different algorithms to generate language with a BERT model. They demonstrate that BERT even though not being trained on an explicit language generation objective, is capable of generating coherent, varied language.

| Language | BERT | Test acc. | Baseline |
|---|---|---|---|
| English | mono | 86.03 | 54.93 |
| | multi | 87.82 | 54.44 |
| German | mono | 97.27 | 69.61 |
| | multi | 95.29 | 69.19 |
| Danish | multi | 89.96 | 53.25 |
| Finnish | multi | 93.20 | 50.54 |
| Nor. (Bokmål) | multi | 93.67 | 56.19 |
| Nor. (Nynorsk) | multi | 94.44 | 53.18 |
| Swedish | multi | 93.00 | 62.09 |

Table 1: Diagnostic classifier results. Auxiliary classification task accuracies and majority class baselines for all languages.

## 3 Experiments

We evaluate the BERT models on 6 languages, English, German, Swedish, Finnish, Danish, and Norwegian (Bokmål and Nynorsk), and three different tasks. In addition to automatic metrics, the generated output is manually evaluated for English, German, Swedish, and Finnish, the four languages that at least one of the authors is fluent in, and therefore comfortable evaluating. For English and German there are monolingual BERT models available, which we use as references to evaluate the performance of the multilingual BERT model.[2] We further compare performance among these languages and the four Nordic languages in order to assess its utility for such relatively low-resource languages. In all evaluation tasks, we use data from the Universal Dependencies (UD) ver 2.4 treebanks (Nivre et al., 2016, 2019) for the languages in question.[3]

### 3.1 Diagnostic Classifier

As an initial experiment, we train a diagnostic classifier to predict whether an auxiliary is the main auxiliary of its sentence, in order to assess how well the BERT encodings represent elementary linguistic information including hierarchical understanding of a sentence. The task is inspired by Lin et al. (2019) who use it as one way of testing what kind of linguistic knowledge BERT

[2]For multilingual and English monolingual experiments we used the official models by the original BERT authors, namely `bert-base-multilingual-cased` and `bert-base-uncased`. For German monolingual experiments we use the model provided by Deepset (`bert-base-german-cased`).

[3]Treebanks are English-EWT, German-HDT (part a), Swedish-Talbanken, Finnish-TDT, Danish-DDT, Norwegian-Bokmaal, and Norwegian-Nynorsk.

is able to encode. Specifically, they use it as a proxy for assessing whether BERT has a hierarchical representation of sentences, as it is necessary information for differentiating between main and subordinate clause or coordinate clause auxiliaries.

All words marked with the part-of-speech tag AUX in the treebank data are taken as prediction candidates, where the target is a binary classification as to whether the auxiliary is dependent on the root token of the sentence or not. The input of the classifier is the final-layer BERT embedding for the auxiliary. In case the auxiliary token is tokenized into multiple subword units, each subword representation is fed as a separate instance, and thus classified independently. We expect each subword embedding to encode the relevant knowledge of both the whole word and its function in the sentence.

The classifier consists of 768 input units corresponding to the BERT base embedding size and a softmax layer. The model is trained separately for all languages and available BERT model configurations, using treebank training sections, and SGD otimizer for 50 epochs. For improved comparability, the train set size is capped for all languages to that of the smallest treebank (Swedish), for which we were able to extract 3031 training examples. The treebank test sets yield 1002–1217 examples, with the exception of Danish with 515 examples.

The results evaluated on the treebank test sets are listed in Table 1, where we measure subword classification accuracy. The majority class baseline frequencies are listed as reference; they tend to be relatively balanced, although somewhat tilted towards main auxiliaries. There is a notable 2 percentage point decrease for German with multilingual BERT, whereas English exhibits a 1.8 point increase. Comparison between languages is problematic, but we observe that all perform relatively well on the task.[4] Albeit our results not being directly comparable with Lin et al., our findings are in line with their work, indicating BERT being able to encode hierarchical sentence information in all languages, and most interestingly, the same holds also for the multilingual BERT model.

[4]The slight variation in baseline between models for the same language is likely influenced by differing tokenization.

| | Mono | Multi |
|---|---|---|
| English | **45.92** | 33.94 |
| German | **43.93** | 28.10 |
| Swedish | | 22.30 |
| Finnish | | 14.56 |
| Danish | | 25.07 |
| Norwegian (Bokmål) | | 25.21 |
| Norwegian (Nynorsk) | | 22.28 |

Table 2: Results for the cloze test in terms of subword predictions accuracy.

### 3.2 Cloze Test

Moving towards natural language generation, and to evaluate the BERT models with respect to their original training objective, we employ a cloze test, where words are randomly masked and predicted back. We mask a random 15% of words in each sentence, and, in case a word is composed of several subwords, all subwords are masked for an easier and more meaningful evaluation. All masked positions are predicted at once in the same manner as done in the BERT pretraining (i.e. no iterative prediction of one position per time step). As a source of sentences, we use the training sections of the treebanks, limited to sentences of 5–50 tokens in length.

The results are shown in Table 2, where we measure subword level prediction accuracy, i.e. how many times the model gives the highest confidence score for the original subword. Overall, we find that the multilingual model substantially lags behind the monolingual variants (at 15–34% vs. 44–45% accuracy), even though the performance at worst is far from trivial. We also observe a notable difference in performance of the multilingual model across the languages, being able to correctly predict between 15% and 34% of the masked subwords. English and German score highest also in the multilingual setting, whereas the Scandinavian languages perform somewhat worse, but similarly among themselves. Finnish stands out as the most challenging.

In order to gain a better understanding of the predictions, we perform a manual evaluation on four languages to observe whether the model is able to fill the gaps with plausible predictions although differing from the original. We manually categorize each predicted word into one of the following categories:

| | | match | mismatch | copy | gibb |
|---|---|---|---|---|---|
| Eng | mono | **88%** | 9% | 1% | 1% |
| | multi | **72%** | 15% | 8% | 6% |
| Ger | mono | **82%** | 12% | 1% | 5% |
| | multi | **69%** | 15% | 6% | 10% |
| Fin | multi | **42%** | 15% | 3% | 39% |
| Swe | multi | **56%** | 19% | 2% | 23% |

Table 3: Manual evaluation of words generated in the cloze test.

| | | on-top | off-top | copy | gibb |
|---|---|---|---|---|---|
| Eng | mono | **50%** | 21% | 5% | 24% |
| | multi | 7% | 2% | 38% | **53%** |
| Ger | mono | **67%** | 28% | 3% | 2% |
| | multi | 17% | 13% | **48%** | 22% |
| Fin | multi | 19% | 2% | 37% | **43%** |
| Swe | multi | 10% | 5% | **47%** | 37% |

Table 4: Manual evaluation of generated text from the mono- and multilingual models. The categories are, in order, on-topic original text, off-topic original text, copy of the context, and gibberish. N is 55–60 for all tests.

- **match:** A real word fitting the context both grammatically and semantically
- **mismatch:** A real word that does not fit the context
- **copy:** An unnatural repetition of a word appearing in the nearby context
- **gibberish:** Subwords do not form a real word, or the prediction forms a meaningless sequence of tokens (e.g. sequence of punctuation tokens)

An example prediction of each category is given in Figure 1 and the evaluation results are summarized in Table 3. These even further demonstrate the capability of the monolingual models, with 82–88% of the generated words fitting the context both syntactically and semantically, i.e. being an acceptable substitution for the masked word in the given context.

By contrast, the matches decrease for German and English, using the multilingual model, to 69% and 72% respectively. Finnish and Swedish perform significantly worse, with match rates at 42% and 56%. The evaluation is based on 50–100 sentences per language and model, and about 100–200 predicted words in each case.

The other categories display similar trends: the semantically or syntactically mismatching words increase for the multilingual model, and in particular the amount of gibberish surges for the Nordic languages. The fact that prediction in Finnish exhibits almost twice as much gibberish as in Swedish is likely influenced by the morphological richness of Finnish, resulting in words to generally be composed of more subword units and the likelihood of predicting non-existent words being higher. An interesting trend for the two Nordic languages, especially strongly seen in Finnish, is the predictions mostly falling into two distinct ends of the evaluation scale, 42% being perfectly acceptable substitutions, while 39% being gibberish. The likely explanation noticed during manual evaluation is the model being quite capable predicting natural output in the place of masked function words, while completely failing to predict anything reasonable for masked content words forming longer subword sequences.

Examples of the model predictions in this task are given in Figure 2 for English, German, Swedish and Finnish, generated using both monolingual and multilingual models.

## 4 Sentence Generation

To evaluate and compare the text generation abilities of the models, we employ the method recently introduced by Wang and Cho (2019) which enables BERT to be used for text generation.[5] In particular, we use the Gibbs-sampling-based method, reported in the paper to give the best results. In this method, a sequence of `[MASK]` symbols is generated and BERT is used for a number of iterations to generate new subwords at random individual positions of this sequence until the maximum number of iterations (500 by default), or convergence are reached. This method is shown by Wang and Cho to produce varied output of good quality, even though not entirely competitive with the famous GPT-2 model (Radford et al., 2019). Most importantly for our objective, this method allows us to probe the model's ability to generate longer sequences of the language and to compare the relative differences between the monolingual and multilingual pre-trained BERT models.

[5]Note that some of the underlying assumptions of this paper were later corrected by the authors `http://tiny.cc/cho-correction`

| Labels | Generated |
|---|---|
| match | Question**[ing~about]** the sinking of the Titanic? |
| mismatch | Those **[they~ones]** are quite small. |
| match, copy | I **[felt~understand]** that it is a **[process~competitive]** process... |
| gibberish | A full **[- of and~substantive]** reconciliation of cash and funding accounts |

Figure 1: Example generation of each category used in the manual evaluation of Cloze task predictions. Examples are generated by the English multilingual model. The format of the masked words is [predicted~gold]. Examples for other languages and models are shown in Figure 2.

| Lang | Model | Generation |
|---|---|---|
| Eng | mono | regarding **[the~those]** rumors about **[people~wolves]** living in yellowstone prior to the official reintroduction? |
| | multi | Regarding **[the~those]** rumors about **[thes~wolves]** living in Yellowstone prior to the official reintroduction? |
| | mono | we **[went~got]** to **[work~talking]** and he got me set up and i **[just~test]** drove with craig and i fell head over heels for this car **[and~all]** i kept saying, "**[but~was]** i gotta have it **[.~!]**" |
| | multi | We **[went~got]** to **[Craig~talking]** and he got me set up and I **[went~test]** drove with Craig and I fell head over heels for this car **[and~all]** I kept saying, "**[And~was]** I gotta have it **[.~!]**" |
| Ger | mono | **[Voraussetzung~Kennzeichen]** für eine **[intensivere~krankhafte]** Nutzung des Internets sei unter anderem ein deutlicher Rückzug **[aus~aus]** dem sozialen Leben. |
| | multi | **[Ein Vorsetzung~Kennzeichen]** für eine **[gewise~krankhafte]** Nutzung des Internets sei unter anderem ein deutlicher Rückzug **[aus~aus]** dem sozialen Leben. |
| | mono | "**[Es~Das]** ist eine Revolution für die mobile Kommunikation", meint **[Professor~Vizepräsident]** Mike Zafirovski. |
| | multi | "**[Es~Das]** ist eine Revolution für die mobile Kommunikation", meint **[der -er~Vizepräsident]** Mike Zafirovski. |
| Fin | multi | Stokessa Gallagher **[oli~pelasi]** enimmäkseen laiturina, joka ei ollut hänen **[valäääa~lempipaikkojaan]**. |
| | multi | Nykyhetki laajenee vauhdilla, joka **[johtaa~saa]** tulevaisuuden kutistumaan lähes menneisyyden kaltaiseksi **[. .ksi . . , ,~makrokääpiöksi]** **[joka~joka]** vierittää kvarkkia alas leskenlehden terää salaiseen maailmaansa. |
| Swe | multi | Men du **[måste~kan]** få ett givande grepp på staden **[från~och]** dess **[, och~miljö]** också från andra utgångspunkter. |
| | multi | År 1951 **[stod~gjorde]** den engelske **[psnologen .~läkaren]** J. Bowlby för WHO:s **[forsknings för en~räkning]** en sammanställning av dittills gjorda undersökningar över hur **[barnär barn~späda]** och små barn, som för någon tid helt skilts **[från~från]** sin mor, utvecklas. |

Figure 2: Example generations of the cloze prediction task for English, German, Finnish and Swedish. The format of the masked words is [predicted~gold].

| Model | Judgement | Generated text in context |
|---|---|---|
| Mono | on-topic | It came out better than I even imagined . **how did this tattoo artist come up with the idea of a quality tattoo ?** I would highly recommend this shop to anyone looking to get a quality tattoo done . |
| Multi | copy | It came out better than I even imagined . **. . this shop to anyone looking to get a quality tattoo done .** I would highly recommend this shop to anyone looking to get a quality tattoo done . |
| Mono | on-topic | Halbleiter-Riese National hatte die zwei Jahre zuvor akquirierte Chipschmiede Cyrix kürzlich an den taiwanischen Chipsatzproduzenten VIA weiter verkauft . **VIA ist die weltweit tätige Tochter von Cyrix ( GM ) .** 130-Nanometer-Chipfertigung läuft an |
| Multi | copy | Halbleiter-Riese National hatte die zwei Jahre zuvor akquirierte Chipschmiede Cyrix kürzlich an den taiwanischen Chipsatzproduzenten VIA weiter verkauft . **128 - Nanometer - Chipfertigung läuft an - an - an .** 130-Nanometer-Chipfertigung läuft an |
| Multi | on-topic | Keskuspankki sitoi Islannin kruunun kurssin euroon kaksi päivää sitten , jolloin eurolla sai 131 kruunua . **1900 - luvun alkuvuonna eurolla sai 140 kruunua .** Käytännössä tämä merkitsi vakavaa iskua Islannin taloudelle . |
| Multi | on-topic | I stadsmiljön utgör parker och grönområden en viktig del i våra dagar . **Stallar i naturen utgör också en viktig del i våra dagar .** Men naturen låg i omedelbar närhet , och stallar och ladugårdar var långt in på 1800-talet vanliga i den agrara svenska småstaden |

Figure 3: Example sentence generations (in bold) together with the manual quality judgements and the context provided in generation, for English, German, Finnish and Swedish.

For each language, we randomly sample 30 documents from the Universal Dependencies version 2.4 training data, and from each document we randomly select 2 sentences. For each of these sentences, we provide on input the preceding and following sentence as the left and right context for the model. Between these contexts, we use the parallel-sequential method of Wang and Cho to generate text which is as long, in terms of subword count, as the original sentence, restricting nevertheless to a minimum of 5 subwords and a maximum of 15 subwords. The maximum of 15 subwords was selected in preliminary experiments, as for considerably longer sequences, the model starts deviating from the seeded context and often fails to even stick to the language of the seed, owing to the fact that BERT is not trained to deal with long sequences of consecutive masked positions.

Subsequently, we manually evaluate the generated texts in context, and classify them into the following categories:

- **on-topic**: original, intelligible sentence or phrase without excessive errors, essentially fitting the context
- **off-topic**: original, intelligible sentence or phrase without excessive errors, not fitting the context
- **copy**: unoriginal text composed for the most part of verbatim copied sections of the context, often containing grammatical and flow errors
- **gibberish**: unintelligible sequence of words and characters, text with excessive grammatical and flow errors

The results of the evaluation are shown in Table 4. A comparison against an existing monolingual model is possible only for English and German. Both for English and German, there is a striking difference, where the monolingual models generate a substantially larger proportion of original on-topic text, compared to the multilingual model which, for the most part, copies sections of the context or produces gibberish. Especially for German, the monolingual model generates a subjectively very good output, with next to no copying and gibberish. For Finnish and Swedish, we can only report on the multilingual model, showing the same tendencies to copy or produce gibberish as for English and German. Overall, the results in Table 4 demonstrate that the multilingual model is clearly inferior to the monolingual counterparts and unsuitable for the generation task.

Figure 3 lists a few examples of generated sentences for the four languages and the available models. For English and German it illustrates the comparably worse performance of the multilingual model, as the generation is mostly copying from the context rather than creating original and fluent text that fits the context. For Finnish and Swedish, it shows cases where the generation has been able to fill in sentences that are correct and that to some extent relates to the context.

## 5 Discussion and Conclusions

In this paper, we set out to establish whether the multilingual BERT model, as distributed, is of sufficient quality to be considered an effective substitute for a dedicated, monolingual model for the given language. We tested the model on three tasks of increasing difficulty: a simple syntactic classification task, a cloze test, and full text generation. We found that the multilingual model notably lags behind the available monolingual models and the gap opens as the complexity of the task increases. While on the syntactic classification task, all models perform comparatively well, in the cloze test there is a notable difference. In the full text generation the multilingual model outputs are practically useless, while the monolingual models produce very good, and in the case of German rather impressive output. We can also observe major differences across languages in the multilingual model where, for instance, in the cloze test the model is considerably more likely to produce gibberish in Finnish than e.g. in German. It is not clear, however, to what extent this reflects the simple fact that Finnish has fewer "easy" functional words, providing for a harder task.

These results allow us to conclude that the current multilingual BERT model as distributed is not able to substitute a well-trained monolingual model in more challenging tasks. This, however, is unlikely due to the multilinguality of the model, rather, we believe it is due to the simple fact that each language is a mere 1/100th of the training data and training effort of the model. In other words, the model seems undertrained w.r.t. to individual languages. This is, for example, hinted at in the text generation task where the multilingual model mostly copies from the context or produces gibberish, while the monolingual models produce a considerably higher proportion of original text. Intuitively, this would fit a pattern where one would expect the model, as it is being trained, to first produce gibberish, then learn to understand and copy, and finally learn to generate.

The primary practical conclusion of this paper is that it is indeed necessary to invest the necessary computational effort to produce well-trained BERT models for other languages instead of relying on the present multilingual model as distributed. We also established baseline results on several tasks across several languages, allowing a better intuitive estimation of the applicability of the multilingual model in different situations.

## Acknowledgments

We gratefully acknowledge the support of the Google Digital News Innovation Fund, Academy of Finland, CSC – IT Center for Science, and the NVIDIA Corporation GPU Grant Program.

## References

Kevin Clark, Urvashi Khandelwal, Omer Levy, and Christopher D. Manning. 2019. https://www.aclweb.org/anthology/W19-4828 What does BERT look at? an analysis of BERT's attention. In *Proceedings of the 2019 ACL Workshop BlackboxNLP: Analyzing and Interpreting Neural Networks for NLP*, pages 276–286, Florence, Italy. Association for Computational Linguistics.

Jacob Devlin, Ming-Wei Chang, Kenton Lee, and Kristina Toutanova. 2018. Bert: Pre-training of deep bidirectional transformers for language understanding. *arXiv preprint arXiv:1810.04805*.

Allyson Ettinger. 2019. What bert is not: Lessons from a new suite of psycholinguistic diagnostics for language models. *arXiv preprint arXiv:1907.13528*.

Yoav Goldberg. 2019. Assessing bert's syntactic abilities. *arXiv preprint arXiv:1901.05287*.

Ganesh Jawahar, Benoît Sagot, and Djamé Seddah. 2019. https://www.aclweb.org/anthology/P19-1356 What does BERT learn about the structure of language? In *Proceedings of the 57th Annual Meeting of the Association for Computational Linguistics*, pages 3651–3657, Florence, Italy. Association for Computational Linguistics.

Yongjie Lin, Yi Chern Tan, and Robert Frank. 2019. Open sesame: Getting inside bert's linguistic knowledge. In *Proceedings of the Second BlackboxNLP*

*Workshop on Analyzing and Interpreting Neural Networks for NLP*.

Joakim Nivre, Mitchell Abrams, Željko Agić, Lars Ahrenberg, Gabrielė Aleksandravičiūtė, Lene Antonsen, Katya Aplonova, Maria Jesus Aranzabe, Gashaw Arutie, Masayuki Asahara, et al. 2019. http://hdl.handle.net/11234/1-2988 Universal dependencies 2.4. LINDAT/CLARIN digital library at the Institute of Formal and Applied Linguistics (ÚFAL), Faculty of Mathematics and Physics, Charles University.

Joakim Nivre, Marie-Catherine De Marneffe, Filip Ginter, Yoav Goldberg, Jan Hajic, Christopher D Manning, Ryan McDonald, Slav Petrov, Sampo Pyysalo, Natalia Silveira, et al. 2016. Universal dependencies v1: A multilingual treebank collection. In *Proceedings of the Tenth International Conference on Language Resources and Evaluation (LREC 2016)*, pages 1659–1666.

Telmo Pires, Eva Schlinger, and Dan Garrette. 2019. https://www.aclweb.org/anthology/P19-1493 How multilingual is multilingual BERT? In *Proceedings of the 57th Annual Meeting of the Association for Computational Linguistics*, pages 4996–5001, Florence, Italy. Association for Computational Linguistics.

Alec Radford, Jeff Wu, Rewon Child, David Luan, Dario Amodei, and Ilya Sutskever. 2019. Language models are unsupervised multitask learners.

Ian Tenney, Dipanjan Das, and Ellie Pavlick. 2019. https://www.aclweb.org/anthology/P19-1452 BERT rediscovers the classical NLP pipeline. In *Proceedings of the 57th Annual Meeting of the Association for Computational Linguistics*, pages 4593–4601, Florence, Italy. Association for Computational Linguistics.

Ashish Vaswani, Noam Shazeer, Niki Parmar, Jakob Uszkoreit, Llion Jones, Aidan N Gomez, Ł ukasz Kaiser, and Illia Polosukhin. 2017. http://papers.nips.cc/paper/7181-attention-is-all-you-need.pdf Attention is all you need. In I. Guyon, U. V. Luxburg, S. Bengio, H. Wallach, R. Fergus, S. Vishwanathan, and R. Garnett, editors, *Advances in Neural Information Processing Systems 30*, pages 5998–6008. Curran Associates, Inc.

Alex Wang and Kyunghyun Cho. 2019. http://arxiv.org/abs/1902.04094 Bert has a mouth, and it must speak: Bert as a markov random field language model.

Shijie Wu and Mark Dredze. 2019. Beto, bentz, becas: The surprising cross-lingual effectiveness of bert. *arXiv preprint arXiv:1904.09077*.

# Multilingual Probing of Deep Pre-Trained Contextual Encoders

**Vinit Ravishankar**
Language Technology Group
Department of Informatics
University of Oslo
vinitr@ifi.uio.no

**Memduh Gökırmak**
Institute of Formal and Applied Linguistics
Faculty of Mathematics and Physics
Charles University in Prague
memduhg@gmail.com

**Lilja Øvrelid**
Language Technology Group
Department of Informatics
University of Oslo
liljao@ifi.uio.no

**Erik Velldal**
Language Technology Group
Department of Informatics
University of Oslo
erikve@ifi.uio.no

## Abstract

Encoders that generate representations based on context have, in recent years, benefited from adaptations that allow for pre-training on large text corpora. Earlier work on evaluating fixed-length sentence representations has included the use of 'probing' tasks, that use diagnostic classifiers to attempt to quantify the extent to which these encoders capture specific linguistic phenomena. The principle of probing has also resulted in extended evaluations that include relatively newer word-level pre-trained encoders. We build on probing tasks established in the literature and comprehensively evaluate and analyse – from a typological perspective amongst others – multilingual variants of existing encoders on probing datasets constructed for 6 non-English languages. Specifically, we probe each layer of a multiple monolingual RNN-based ELMo models, the transformer-based BERT's cased and uncased multilingual variants, and a variant of BERT that uses a cross-lingual modelling scheme (XLM).

## 1 Introduction

Recent trends in NLP have demonstrated the utility of pre-trained deep contextual representations in numerous downstream NLP tasks, where they have almost consistently resulted in significant performance improvements. Detailed evaluations have naturally followed: these have either been follow-up works to papers describing contextual representation systems, such as Peters et al. (2018b), or novel works evaluating a broad class of encoders on a broad variety of tasks (Perone et al., 2018). This paper is an example of the latter sort; we perform a comprehensive, large-scale evaluation of what linguistic phenomena these sequential encoders capture across a diverse set of languages. This has often been referred to in the literature as *probing*; we use this terminology throughout this work.

Briefly, our goals are to probe our encoders in a multilingual setting – i.e., we use a series of probing tasks to quantify what sort of linguistic information our encoders retain, and how this information varies across language, across encoder, and across task. As such, our experiments do not attempt to attain 'state-of-the-art' results; instead, we attempt to use a comparable experimental setting across each experiment, to quantify differences between settings rather than absolute results.

In Section 2, we describe prior work in multiple strands of research: specifically, on deep neural pre-training, on multilingualism in pre-training, and on evaluation. Section 3 describes both the linguistic features we probe our representations for, and how we generated our probing corpus. In Section 4, we describe and motivate our choice of encoders, as well as describe our infrastructural details. The bulk of our contribution is in Section 5, where we describe and analyse our results. Finally, we conclude with a discussion of the implications of these results and future work in Section 6.

## 2 Background

### 2.1 Deep pre-training

A watershed moment in NLP has been the recent innovation spree in deep pre-training; it has represented a considerable step up from shallow pre-training methods, that have been used in NLP since the introduction of contextual word embedding models such as word2vec (Mikolov et al., 2013). Whilst deep pre-training has been used in non-NLP, image-oriented tasks, where the standard paradigm is to pre-train deep convolutional networks on datasets like ImageNet (Russakovsky et al., 2014), and then fine-tune on task-specific data, their introduction to textual domains has been considerably slower, yet has been picking up rapidly in recent years.

An early paper in this theme was CoVe (McCann et al., 2017), that pre-trained contextual encoders on seq2seq machine translation models. Another earlier seminal work that addressed numerous technical issues with pre-training was Howard and Ruder's ULMFiT (2018). Not long after, the principle of deep pre-training saw widespread adoption with ELMo (Peters et al., 2018a), that consisted of several innovations over CoVe: critically, the use of an unsupervised (albeit structured) task – language modelling – for pre-training, and the use of a linear combination of all encoder layers, instead of just the top layer. Architecturally, ELMo used two-layer bidirectional LSTMs along with character-level convolutions, to model word probabilities given the history.

With deep pre-training having been established as a valid strategy in NLP, alternative models with different underlying architectures were proposed. The OpenAI GPT (Radford et al., 2018) was one such model; instead of LSTMs, it used the *de*coder of an attention-based transformer (Vaswani et al., 2017) as its underlying *en*coder – the justification being that using the transformer's *en*coder would lead to each token having access to succeeding tokens. The GPT also achieved (then) state-of-the-art results by plugging generated fixed-length vectors into downstream classifiers.

Another system that represented a significant innovation was BERT (Devlin et al., 2018). BERT introduced a language modelling variant, dubbed *masked* language modelling, that allowed them to use transformer encoders as their underlying encoding mechanism.

### 2.2 Multilingual pre-training

Multilingual variants of pre-trained encoders that provide contextual representations for non-English languages have also been studied; there is, however, some diversity in precisely how they are generated.

Che et al. (2018) provide ELMo models (Fares et al., 2017) for 44 languages; all of these were trained on data provided as part of the CoNLL 2018 shared task on dependency parsing Universal Dependencies treebanks (Zeman et al., 2018). This makes 'multilingual' a bit of a misnomer: whilst this is the most obvious approach to multilingual *support*, these models are all *mono*lingual. This also leads to other issues downstream, such as a complete inability to deal with true multilingual phenomena like code-switching. Throughout this text, however, when not specifically referring to ELMo, our use of the term 'multilingual' is inclusive of ELMo's quasi-multilingualism.

This is contrasted with BERT's approach to (true) multilingualism, which trains a single model that can handle all languages. The authors use WordPiece, a variant of BPE (Sennrich et al., 2016), for tokenisation, using a 110K-size vocabulary, and proceed to train a single gigantic model; they perform exponentially smoothed weighting of their data to avoid biasing their model towards better-resourced languages.

Finally, XLM (Lample and Conneau, 2019) is another cross-lingual encoder based on BERT that implements a number of modifications. Along with BERT's masked language modeling or Cloze task-based modelling (Devlin et al., 2018; Taylor, 1953), XLM training uses another similar objective during training that the authors call translation language modeling. Here, two parallel sentences are concatenated and words masked in both source and target sentences words are predicted using context from both. The authors here also use their own implementation of BPE – FastBPE, for which they provide a vocabulary of around 120K entries. This vocabulary is shared across all of the languages and thus improves the alignment of embedded spaces, as shown in Lample et al. (2017).

### 2.3 On evaluation

Evaluation of contextual representations goes beyond merely deep representations; not too far in the past, work on evaluating shallow sentence representations was encouraged by the release of the SentEval toolkit (Conneau and Kiela, 2018), which provided an easy-to-use framework that sentence representations could be 'plugged' into, for rapid downstream evaluation on numerous tasks: these include several classification tasks, textual entailment and similarity tasks, a paraphrase detection task, and caption/image retrieval tasks. Relevant to our paper is Conneau et al.'s (2018a) set of 'probing tasks', a variant on the theme of diagnostic classification (Hupkes et al., 2017; Belinkov et al., 2017; Adi et al., 2016; Shi et al., 2016), that would attempt to quantify precisely what sort of linguistic information was being retained by sentence representations. Based in part on Shi et al. (2016), Conneau et al. (2018a) focus on evaluating representations for English; they provide Spearman correlations between the performance of a particular representation mechanism on being probed for specific linguistic properties, and the downstream performance on a variety of NLP tasks. Along similar lines, and contemporaneously with this work, Liu et al. (2019) probe similar deep pre-trained to the ones we do, on a set of 'sixteen diverse probing tasks'. (Tenney et al., 2018) probe deep pre-trained encoders for sentence structure.

On a different note, Saphra and Lopez (2018) present a CCA-based method to compare representation learning dynamics across time and models, without explicitly requiring annotated corpora.

A visible limitation of the datasets provided by these probing tasks is that most of them were created with the idea of evaluating representations built for English language data. Within the realm of evaluating *multilingual* sentence representations, Conneau et al. (2018b) describe the XNLI dataset, a set of translations of the development and test portions of the multi-genre MultiNLI inference dataset (Williams et al., 2018). This, in a sense, is an extension of a predominantly monolingual task to the multilingual domain; the authors evaluate sentence representations derived by *mapping* non-English representations to an English representation space.

### 2.4 BERTology

Relevant to the probing theme of this paper is the sudden recent growth in papers studying precisely what is retained with the internal representations of pre-trained encoders like BERT. These include, for instance, analyses of BERT's attentions heads, such as Michel et al. (2019), where the authors prune heads, often reducing certain layers to single heads, without a significant drop in performance in certain scenarios. Clark et al. (2019) provide a per-head analysis and attempt to quantify what information each head retains; they discover that specific aspects of syntax are well-encoded per head, and find heads that correspond to certain linguistic properties, such as heads that attend to direct objects of verbs. Other papers provide analyses of BERT's layers, such as Tenney et al. (2019), who discover that BERT's layers roughly correspond to the notion of the classical 'NLP pipeline', with lower level tasks such as tagging lower down the layer hierarchy. Hewitt and Manning (2019) define a structural probe over BERT representations, that extracts notions of syntax that correspond strongly to linguistic notions of dependency syntax.

## 3 Corpora

### 3.1 Probing

Our data consists of training, development and test splits for 9 linguistic tasks, that can broadly be grouped into surface, syntactic and semantic tasks. These are the same as the ones described in Conneau et al. (2018a), with minor modifications. Due to the differences in corpus domain, we alter some of their word-frequency parameters. We also exclude the top constituent (**TopConst**) task; we noticed that Wikipedia tended to have far less diversity in sentence structure than the original Toronto Books corpus, due to the more encyclopaedic style of writing. A brief description of the tasks follows, although we urge the reader to refer to the original paper for more detailed descriptions.

1. Sentence length: In **SentLen**, sentences are divided into multiple bins based on their length; the job of the classifier is to predict the appropriate bin, creating a 6-way classification task.

2. Word count: In **WC**, we sample sentences that feature exactly one amongst a thousand mid-frequency words, and train the classifier to predict the word: this is the most 'difficult' task, in that it has the most possible classes.

3. Tree depth: The **TreeDepth** task simply asks the representation to predict the depth of the sentence's syntax tree. Unlike the original

paper, we use the depth the of the dependency tree instead of the constituency tree.

4. Bigram shift: In **BiShift**, for half the sentences in the dataset, the order of words in a randomly sampled bigram is reversed. The classifier learns to predict whether or not the sentence contains a reversal.

5. Subject number: The **SubjNum** task asks the classifier to predict the number of the subject of the head verb of the sentence. Only sentences with exactly one subject (annotated with the `nsubj` relation) attached to the root verb were considered.

6. Object number: **ObjNum**, similar to the subject number task, was annotated with the number of the direct object of the head verb (annotated with the `obj` relation).

7. Coordination inversion: In **CoordInv**, two main clauses joined by a coordinating conjunction have their orders reversed, with a probability of one in two. Only sentences with exactly two top-level conjuncts are considered.

8. (Semantic) odd man out: **SOMO**, one of the more difficult tasks in the collection, replaces a randomly sampled word with another word with comparable corpus bigram frequencies.

9. Tense prediction: The **Tense** prediction asks the classifier to predict the tense of the main verb: we compare the past and present tenses.

### 3.2 Data

#### Languages

Our choice of languages was motivated by three factors: i) the availability of a Wikipedia large enough to extract data from; ii) the availability of a reasonable dependency parsing model, and iii) typological diversity. The former, in particular, was a bit of a restriction, since not all sentences were valid candidates for extraction per task. Our final set of languages include an additional corpus for English, as well as French, German, Spanish, Russian, Turkish and Finnish. Whilst not nearly representative of the diversity of world languages, this selection includes morphologically agglutinative, fusional and (relatively) isolating languages, and it includes two scripts, Latin and Cyrillic. The languages also represent three families (Indo-European, Turkic and Uralic).

We build our probing datasets using the relevant language's Wikipedia dump as a corpus. Our motivation for doing so was that it a freely available corpus for numerous languages, large enough to extract the sizeable corpora that we need. Specifically, we use Wikipedia dumps (dated 2019-02-01), which we process using the WikiExtractor utility[1].

#### Preprocessing

We use the Punkt tokeniser (Kiss and Strunk, 2006) to segment our Wikipedia dumps into discrete sentences. For Russian, which lacked a Punkt tokenisation model, we used the UDPipe (Straka and Straková, 2017) toolkit to perform segmentation.

Having segmented our data, we used the Moses (Koehn et al., 2007) tokeniser for the appropriate language, falling back to English tokenisation when unavailable.

Next, we obtained dependency parses for our sentences, again using the UDPipe toolkit's pretrained models, trained on Universal Dependencies treebanks (Nivre et al., 2015). We then processed these dependency parsed corpora to extract the appropriate sentences; while in principle, each task was meant to have 120K sentences, with 100K/10K/10K training/validation/test splits, often, for the rarer linguistic phenomena, we ran out of source data, in particular with Turkish and Finnish, although to a smaller extent with Russian as well. In these situations, we ensured an equivalent split ratio.

Our use of non-gold-standard dependency parses implies inaccuracies that, in principle, would propagate to our training data. A valid counterargument, however, is that we do not rely on complete parse accuracies for all our tasks; several tasks do not require dependency or POS annotation, and the ones that do rely on a fixed subset of dependency relations, such as `nsubj` or `obj`. Having said that, we do acknowledge the divergences in parsing performance across language; unfortunately, given the substantial corpus sizes these experiments require, we could not use gold-standard parsed corpora.

[1] `https://github.com/attardi/wikiextractor/`

## 4 Implementation

### 4.1 Encoders

We probe several popular pre-trained encoders (or, specifically, their multilingual variants). These include:

**ELMo, monolingual** We use Che et al.'s (2018) pre-trained monolingual ELMo models for each of our languages. Training was similar to the original English language ELMo, but allows for Unicode, and uses a sample softmax (Jean et al., 2014) to deal with large vocabularies. We probed four variants of each ELMo model - the character embeddings layer, the two LSTM layers, and an average of all three. For obtaining a fixed-length sentence representation, we use average pooling over the sequence of hidden states.

**BERT** We use the two multilingual variants - cased and uncased. Both variants have 12 layers, 768 hidden units, 12 heads and 110M parameters; the former includes 104 languages and fixes normalisation issues, whilst the latter includes 102 languages. For further classification, we use the first hidden state, represented by the `[CLS]` token.

**XLM** We probe only one variant of this encoder - i.e., the models fine-tuned on XNLI (Conneau et al., 2018b) data. Due to there being no XNLI data for Finnish, we do not probe our Finnish dataset with XLM. Unlike BERT, XLM uses 1024 hidden units and 8 heads.

Unfortunately, all our encoders did include Wikipedia dumps in their training data. Given that pretrained encoders tend to use as much easily accessible data as possible in pre-training, however, it is difficult to avoid using a completely unseen corpus for probing task extraction.

### 4.2 Implementation

Our probing procedure for each of our languages and encoders is relatively similar: we use a multilayer perceptron based classifier to assign the appropriate class label to each input sentence. During training, the encoders remain static, with all learning restricted to the classifier. In an attempt to avoid excessively complex classifiers, and to ensure consistency across tasks and languages, we use predetermined fixed hyperparameters – specifically, a sigmoid activation function, on top of a size 50 dense layer. We use a training batch size of 32, optimised using Adam (Kingma and Ba, 2014), and train for 10 epochs, allowing for early stopping.

We implement our system using the AllenNLP toolkit (Gardner et al., 2018), which crucially provides the ability to use the appropriate tokenisation schema, along with the appropriate vocabulary, for each encoder. Training and evaluation were carried out on NVIDIA RTX 2080 Ti GPUs, with 10GiB GPU memory.

## 5 Results

Due to our large experiment space, there are several dimensions along which our results can be analysed and discussed. For ease of analysis, all our figures are presented as heatmaps.

We have presented our results in two ways, for easy visualisation. The first of these is dividing them up by task, as in Figure 1. We present an alternative set of results for three of our encoders, in Figure 2.

### 5.1 Encoder

An observation that instantly stands out is the significant difference in performance on WC: consistently, across every language, all our transformer-based architectures see results very close to 0. Further, whilst not instantly visible in Figure 2, a quick look at Figure 1 shows that the same appears to hold (albeit to a lesser extent) for SentLen, TreeDepth and BiShift, all of which are either surface or syntactic phenomena. This appears to heavily imply that recurrent, sequential processing appears to retain lower level linguistic phenomena better than self-attentive mechanisms (that do not see the same drop in informativity for semantic tasks). This is perhaps a bit easy to justify with SentLen, which is a phenomenon that is directly proportional to recurrence depth.

The next phenomenon of interest is the difference between each of ELMo's layers. Interestingly, these do not appear to be as drastic as one would imagine, given the differences in performance on downstream tasks. The difference between raw word representations and actual contextual representations is fairly noticeable, particularly on the strongly syntactic BiShift. However, the differences between higher layers is rela-

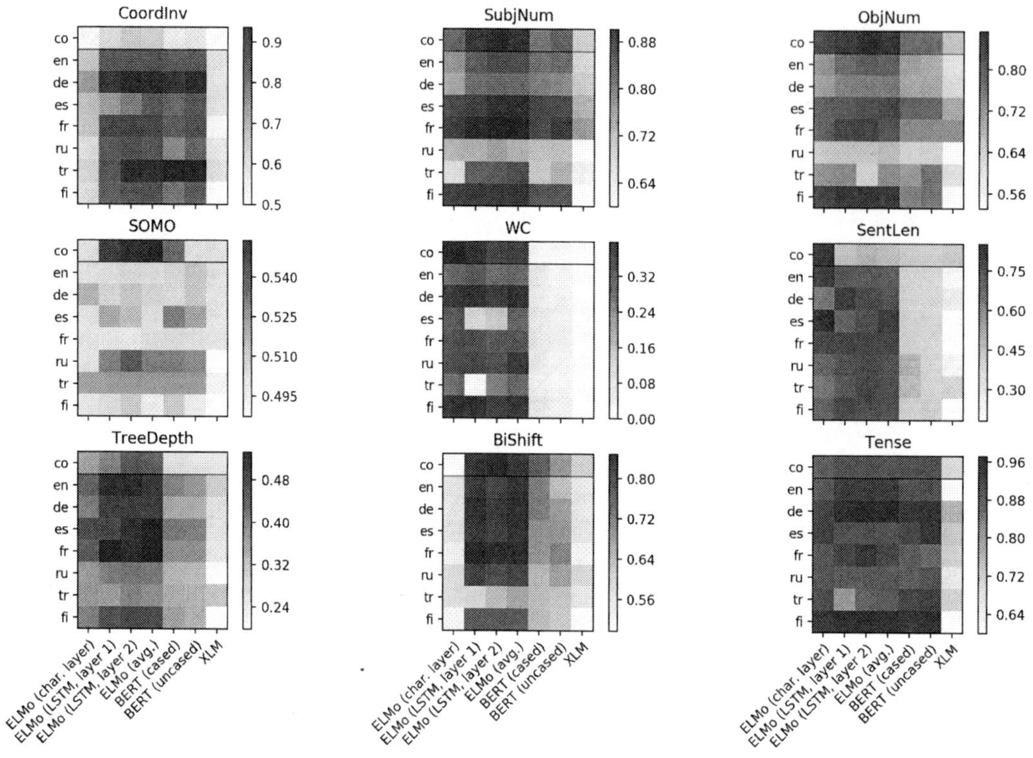


Figure 1: Detailed results per task, per language per encoder. Each task's result heatmap has its own scale. All results mentioned in this paper refer to classification accuracies in [0.0, 1.0]. Henceforth, 'co' refers to probing results on Conneau et al.'s (2018a) original corpus.

tively murkier, and whilst the average of the three does appear to represent some phenomena better (such as CoordInv), it isn't clear that this difference is meaningful. Notably, SentLen appears to be poorly represented in higher layers, which ties in with other analyses of ELMo (Peters et al., 2018b), that imply that higher layers are likelier to learn more semantic features.

BERT's cased variant appears to retain information slightly better than the uncased one, which is in line with the authors' descriptions of their own models.

Finally, and perhaps most interestingly, we turn our attention towards XLM. Despite being based on BERT (and indeed showing similar *patterns* in performance), XLM appears to perform a lot worse than all our other encoders on virtually every task. It is not immediately clear why: however, given that this drop in performance is visible in every language, our conjecture is that due to the translation-based modelling employed by XLM, the encoder does indeed succeed at learning language-independent representations, or 'universal' representations. However, this universality comes at a cost: in an attempt to adequately represent a variety of typologically diverse languages, XLM appears to lose its ability to retain *specific* linguistic phenomena pertaining to specific languages; in a sense, it is incapable of building a representation for a language that adequately captures a specific phenomenon in that language *and no other*. This follows intuitively from the method used training on the TLM objective: the authors concatenate aligned parallel sentences and predict masked words in the source *and* the target sentence, using context from both sentences at the same time to predict each masked word. This is likely to have had a detrimental effect on XLM's ability to retain characteristics specific to each language. In Figure 3, we show the relative performance of BERT and XLM per probing task. There is a clear trend towards BERT's enhanced retention of linguistic features being less prominent for the more semantic tasks, which fits our hypothesis, as semantics are likelier to hold cross-linguistically.

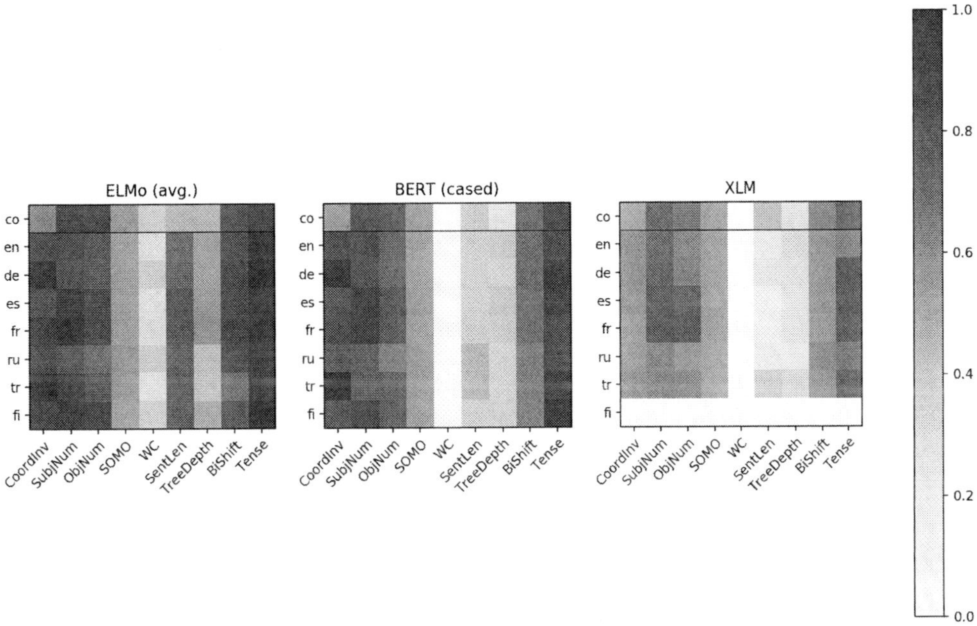


Figure 2: Results for select encoders, per language per task. All results use the same scale, [0.0, 1.0].

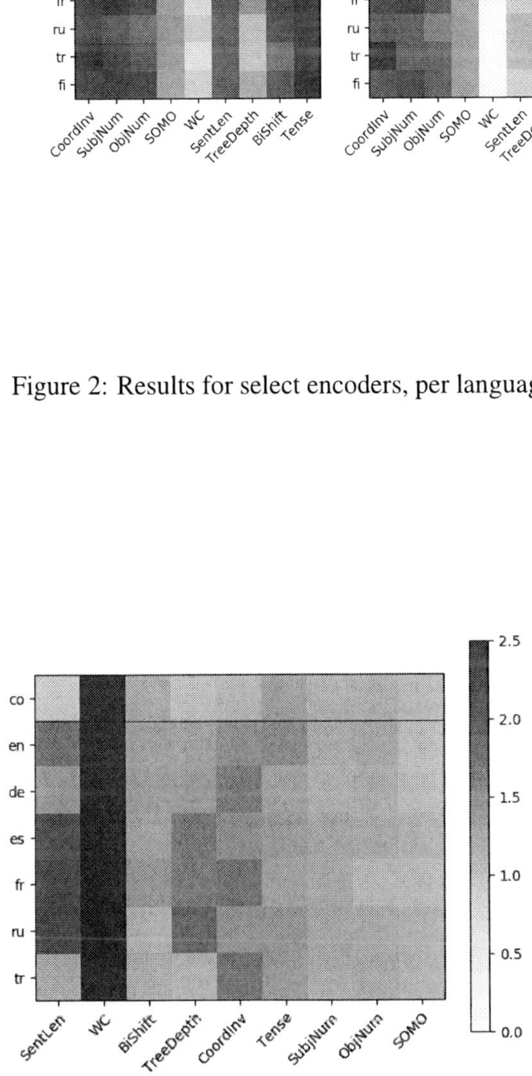


Figure 3: BERT (cased) scores divided by the corresponding XLM scores. Tasks are ordered, from surface to syntax to semantic level tasks.

A point to be made here is that despite SubjNum, ObjNum and Tense being classified as semantic tasks, it isn't clear that they are truly being probed for semantic information: all three phenomena tend to be visible with morphological marking. This gives us an alternative justification for XLM's relative improvement in retention: XLM is likely capable of storing each language's individual morphological information in different internal subspaces de, as each language is likely to reflect morphology purely orthographically, and in mutually exclusive ways.

Our observations on the differences between encoders are also easily visible in Figure 4, where multiple 'belts' of varying performances emerge.

### 5.2 Language

To motivate one of the main focuses of this paper – our analysis of our results along linguistic lines – we present Figure 5, which displays what one might call the net 'informativity' of an encoder, i.e. an average of how much information each encoder retains averaged over tasks. The most noticeable effect here is the drop in informativity for Russian and Turkish. While this is perhaps understandable for Turkish – which has smaller probing corpora, and a less reliable Wikipedia than the other languages – Russian's opaqueness cannot be

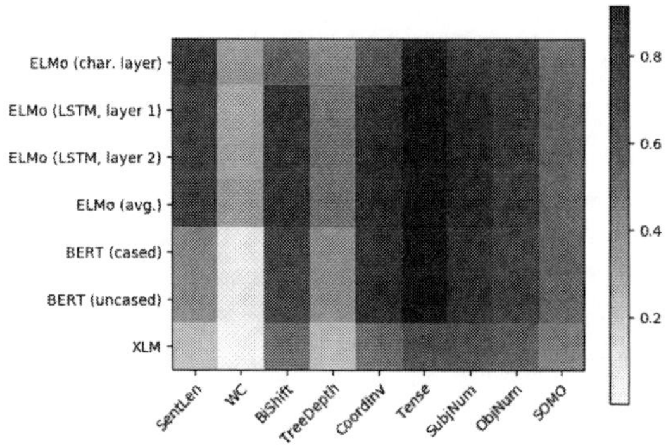


Figure 4: Linguistic information retained per encoder, per task; scores are averaged over language.

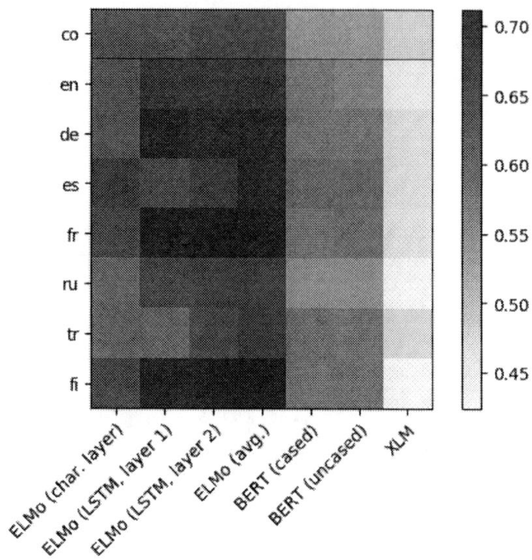


Figure 5: Net encoder 'informativity' per language; results averaged over all tasks.

as easily explained away, particularly when contrasted with Finnish, which tends to have fewer resources.

We further introduce Figure 6, which displays the averaged results of three systems – ELMo's multilayer variant, BERT's cased variant and (absent for Finnish) XLM. Most linguistic differences appear to be clustered in the semantic part of this heatmap. There are numerous possible factors that could explain these divergences, not the least of which is the actual probing corpus itself: however, we attempt to provide a justification, from a typological perspective, for some of these results.

When averaged across encoders, the Tense task stands out as fairly easy to probe for all languages. It thus seems that information about verbal temporal properties is retained in the sentence representation. For the tasks of subject and object number, however, we observe clear differences between the languages. Here, French and Spanish appear to be somewhat easier to probe than other languages. We hypothesise that this is due to both languages marking nominal number, not just with verb agreement, but also with plural articles, resulting in representations that are more informative regarding number. Contrast this with English and German, which either do not have plural articles, or have plural articles that morphologically overlap with non-plural forms, or with Russian, that tends to avoid articles in general.

Other interesting observations are German's relative ability at retaining information on CoordInv and Tense, as well as Finnish's extraordinarily high performance on Tense. Further, SentLen appears to be retained better, counter-intuitively, in Russian, Turkish and Finnish; a brief look at Figure 1 shows that, interestingly, this is likely due to BERT.

Finally, we note that our results do not seem to indicate that English is somehow better represented in our multilingual systems, nor does it appear to perform significantly better than other languages in general, indicating that none of our models are 'learning' English first and then adapting to other languages.

### 5.3 Task

From a monolingual perspective, most of what needs to be said regarding the choice of probing tasks has already been said in the original (Conneau et al., 2018a). There are however several differences, induced both by our modifications to the original framework, and by our corpus's multilingualism.

The first of these is the apparently consistent differences in performance on certain tasks which include, amongst others, CoordInv, where our variant appears to be more easily retained than the original. This can be explained away by minor issues we faced during implementation, using dependency trees instead of constituency trees. Due to more complicated representation of conjuncts in UD-style dependency trees, some of our sentences had issues with using the appropriate casing after swapping conjuncts, as well as ensuring consistent punctuation. While we attempted to avoid these by writing filtering rules, these were imperfect, and it is likely that stray punctuation and the like might have informed our representations about the conjuncts being swapped, in some instances.

Another task with minor differences is our implementation of SOMO; we attribute this to not being able to accurately reproduce Conneau et al.'s (2018a) modified corpus-frequency range (40-400) to adequately fit all our corpora.

We note that there do not appear to be significant differences in the TreeDepth task, despite our using dependency trees instead of constituency, and despite our tree depth/sentence length decorrelation procedure being markedly simpler.

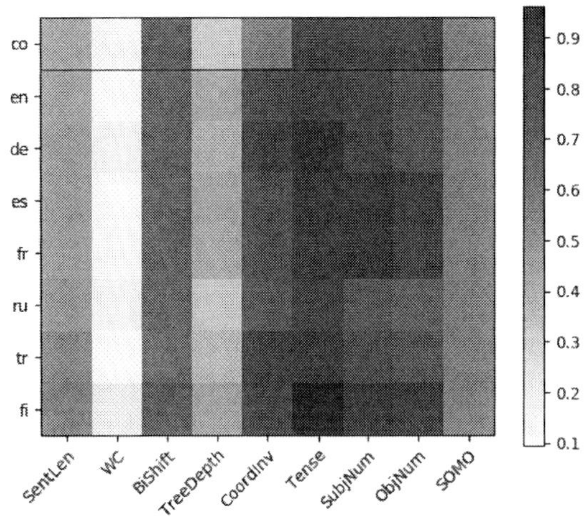


Figure 6: Linguistic insight per language per task, averaged over one variant of every encoder: multi-layer ELMo, cased BERT, and XLM (bar Finnish).

## 6 Discussion

### 6.1 Implications

Having elaborated our results, it becomes crucial to contextualise their importance. 'Probing' an encoder, or more correctly, using diagnostic classifiers to attempt to *quantify* what information an encoder stores, appears to be a reasonable approach to *qualifying* this information. However, there has been some critique of this approach. To paraphrase Saphra and Lopez (2018), the architecture of a diagnostic classifier does affect the performance of a probing task; further, lower layers of encoders may represent information in ways designed to be picked up on by their own higher layers; this might prove difficult for simple classifiers to truly probe.

This is an excellent critique of the principle using *absolute* probing performance, or *absolute* numbers representing performance on an abstract insight task, as a yardstick. Critically, this work is focussed, both practically and in principle, on elucidating *relative* results, in a wide space of languages and encoders. The relative underparameterisation of the classifier and the use of one constant set of hyperparameters across experiments is an attempt to minimise the *relative* interference of the classifier. i.e., our goal is to keep the classifier's interference – its lens – as consistent as possible.

### 6.2 Future work

One potential strand of research relates directly to the tasks themselves: our choice of tasks was fairly restrictive, and does not include many tasks that are truly *semantic*, which does not provide us with enough information to draw conclusions similar to Liu et al. (2019), which is that pretrained models encode stronger syntax than semantics. An obvious goal, therefore, is the more careful design of tasks, particularly within a multilingual context: the tasks proposed by Liu et al. (2019) and Tenney et al. (2018) are not strictly easy to motivate cross-linguistically due to the burden of annotation. This could include more semantic-level probing by means of existing cross-lingual semantic resources, such as the Parallel Meaning Bank (Abzianidze et al., 2017).

## References


Lasha Abzianidze, Johannes Bjerva, Kilian Evang, Hessel Haagsma, Rik van Noord, Pierre Ludmann, Duc-Duy Nguyen, and Johan Bos. 2017. The Parallel Meaning Bank: Towards a Multilingual Corpus of Translations Annotated with Compositional Meaning Representations. *arXiv:1702.03964 [cs]*. ArXiv: 1702.03964.

Yossi Adi, Einat Kermany, Yonatan Belinkov, Ofer Lavi, and Yoav Goldberg. 2016. Fine-grained Analysis of Sentence Embeddings Using Auxiliary Prediction Tasks. *arXiv:1608.04207 [cs]*. ArXiv: 1608.04207.

Yonatan Belinkov, Nadir Durrani, Fahim Dalvi, Hassan Sajjad, and James Glass. 2017. What do Neural Machine Translation Models Learn about Morphology? In *Proceedings of the 55th Annual Meeting of the Association for Computational Linguistics (Volume 1: Long Papers)*, pages 861–872, Vancouver, Canada. Association for Computational Linguistics.

Wanxiang Che, Yijia Liu, Yuxuan Wang, Bo Zheng,

and Ting Liu. 2018. Towards Better UD Parsing: Deep Contextualized Word Embeddings, Ensemble, and Treebank Concatenation. *arXiv:1807.03121 [cs]*. ArXiv: 1807.03121.

Kevin Clark, Urvashi Khandelwal, Omer Levy, and Christopher D Manning. 2019. What does bert look at? an analysis of bert's attention. *arXiv preprint arXiv:1906.04341*.

Alexis Conneau and Douwe Kiela. 2018. SentEval: An Evaluation Toolkit for Universal Sentence Representations. *arXiv:1803.05449 [cs]*. ArXiv: 1803.05449.

Alexis Conneau, German Kruszewski, Guillaume Lample, Loc Barrault, and Marco Baroni. 2018a. What you can cram into a single vector: Probing sentence embeddings for linguistic properties. *arXiv:1805.01070 [cs]*. ArXiv: 1805.01070.

Alexis Conneau, Guillaume Lample, Ruty Rinott, Adina Williams, Samuel R. Bowman, Holger Schwenk, and Veselin Stoyanov. 2018b. XNLI: Evaluating Cross-lingual Sentence Representations. *arXiv:1809.05053 [cs]*. ArXiv: 1809.05053.

Jacob Devlin, Ming-Wei Chang, Kenton Lee, and Kristina Toutanova. 2018. BERT: Pre-training of Deep Bidirectional Transformers for Language Understanding. *arXiv:1810.04805 [cs]*. ArXiv: 1810.04805.

Murhaf Fares, Andrey Kutuzov, Stephan Oepen, and Erik Velldal. 2017. Word vectors, reuse, and replicability: Towards a community repository of large-text resources. In *Proceedings of the 21st Nordic Conference on Computational Linguistics*, pages 271–276, Gothenburg, Sweden. Association for Computational Linguistics.

Matt Gardner, Joel Grus, Mark Neumann, Oyvind Tafjord, Pradeep Dasigi, Nelson Liu, Matthew Peters, Michael Schmitz, and Luke Zettlemoyer. 2018. AllenNLP: A Deep Semantic Natural Language Processing Platform. *arXiv:1803.07640 [cs]*. ArXiv: 1803.07640.

John Hewitt and Christopher D Manning. 2019. A structural probe for finding syntax in word representations. In *Proceedings of the 2019 Conference of the North American Chapter of the Association for Computational Linguistics: Human Language Technologies, Volume 1 (Long and Short Papers)*, pages 4129–4138.

Jeremy Howard and Sebastian Ruder. 2018. Universal Language Model Fine-tuning for Text Classification. *arXiv:1801.06146 [cs, stat]*. ArXiv: 1801.06146.

Dieuwke Hupkes, Sara Veldhoen, and Willem Zuidema. 2017. Visualisation and 'diagnostic classifiers' reveal how recurrent and recursive neural networks process hierarchical structure. *arXiv:1711.10203 [cs]*. ArXiv: 1711.10203.

Sbastien Jean, Kyunghyun Cho, Roland Memisevic, and Yoshua Bengio. 2014. On Using Very Large Target Vocabulary for Neural Machine Translation. *arXiv:1412.2007 [cs]*. ArXiv: 1412.2007.

Diederik P. Kingma and Jimmy Ba. 2014. Adam: A Method for Stochastic Optimization. *arXiv:1412.6980 [cs]*. ArXiv: 1412.6980.

Tibor Kiss and Jan Strunk. 2006. Unsupervised multilingual sentence boundary detection. *Computational Linguistics*, 32(4):485–525.

Philipp Koehn, Hieu Hoang, Alexandra Birch, Chris Callison-Burch, Marcello Federico, Nicola Bertoldi, Brooke Cowan, Wade Shen, Christine Moran, Richard Zens, et al. 2007. Moses: Open source toolkit for statistical machine translation. In *Proceedings of the 45th annual meeting of the association for computational linguistics companion volume proceedings of the demo and poster sessions*, pages 177–180.

Guillaume Lample and Alexis Conneau. 2019. Cross-lingual Language Model Pretraining. *arXiv:1901.07291 [cs]*. ArXiv: 1901.07291.

Guillaume Lample, Ludovic Denoyer, and Marc'Aurelio Ranzato. 2017. Unsupervised machine translation using monolingual corpora only. *CoRR*, abs/1711.00043.

Nelson F Liu, Matt Gardner, Yonatan Belinkov, Matthew E Peters, and Noah A Smith. 2019. Linguistic Knowledge and Transferability of Contextual Representations. page 22.

Bryan McCann, James Bradbury, Caiming Xiong, and Richard Socher. 2017. Learned in Translation: Contextualized Word Vectors. *arXiv:1708.00107 [cs]*. ArXiv: 1708.00107.

Paul Michel, Omer Levy, and Graham Neubig. 2019. Are sixteen heads really better than one? *arXiv preprint arXiv:1905.10650*.

Tomas Mikolov, Ilya Sutskever, Kai Chen, Greg S Corrado, and Jeff Dean. 2013. Distributed Representations of Words and Phrases and their Compositionality. In C. J. C. Burges, L. Bottou, M. Welling, Z. Ghahramani, and K. Q. Weinberger, editors, *Advances in Neural Information Processing Systems 26*, pages 3111–3119. Curran Associates, Inc.

Joakim Nivre, Željko Agić, Maria Jesus Aranzabe, Masayuki Asahara, Aitziber Atutxa, Miguel Ballesteros, John Bauer, Kepa Bengoetxea, Riyaz Ahmad Bhat, Cristina Bosco, Sam Bowman, Giuseppe G. A. Celano, Miriam Connor, Marie-Catherine de Marneffe, Arantza Diaz de Ilarraza, Kaja Dobrovoljc, Timothy Dozat, Tomaž Erjavec, Richárd Farkas, Jennifer Foster, Daniel Galbraith, Filip Ginter, Iakes Goenaga, Koldo Gojenola, Yoav Goldberg, Berta Gonzales, Bruno Guillaume, Jan

Hajič, Dag Haug, Radu Ion, Elena Irimia, Anders Johannsen, Hiroshi Kanayama, Jenna Kanerva, Simon Krek, Veronika Laippala, Alessandro Lenci, Nikola Ljubešić, Teresa Lynn, Christopher Manning, Cătălina Mărănduc, David Mareček, Héctor Martínez Alonso, Jan Mašek, Yuji Matsumoto, Ryan McDonald, Anna Missilä, Verginica Mititelu, Yusuke Miyao, Simonetta Montemagni, Shunsuke Mori, Hanna Nurmi, Petya Osenova, Lilja Øvrelid, Elena Pascual, Marco Passarotti, Cenel-Augusto Perez, Slav Petrov, Jussi Piitulainen, Barbara Plank, Martin Popel, Prokopis Prokopidis, Sampo Pyysalo, Loganathan Ramasamy, Rudolf Rosa, Shadi Saleh, Sebastian Schuster, Wolfgang Seeker, Mojgan Seraji, Natalia Silveira, Maria Simi, Radu Simionescu, Katalin Simkó, Kiril Simov, Aaron Smith, Jan Štěpánek, Alane Suhr, Zsolt Szántó, Takaaki Tanaka, Reut Tsarfaty, Sumire Uematsu, Larraitz Uria, Viktor Varga, Veronika Vincze, Zdeněk Žabokrtský, Daniel Zeman, and Hanzhi Zhu. 2015. Universal dependencies 1.2. LINDAT/CLARIN digital library at the Institute of Formal and Applied Linguistics (ÚFAL), Faculty of Mathematics and Physics, Charles University.

Christian S. Perone, Roberto Silveira, and Thomas S. Paula. 2018. Evaluation of sentence embeddings in downstream and linguistic probing tasks. *arXiv:1806.06259 [cs]*. ArXiv: 1806.06259.

Matthew E. Peters, Mark Neumann, Mohit Iyyer, Matt Gardner, Christopher Clark, Kenton Lee, and Luke Zettlemoyer. 2018a. Deep contextualized word representations. *arXiv:1802.05365 [cs]*. ArXiv: 1802.05365.

Matthew E. Peters, Mark Neumann, Luke Zettlemoyer, and Wen-tau Yih. 2018b. Dissecting Contextual Word Embeddings: Architecture and Representation. *arXiv:1808.08949 [cs]*. ArXiv: 1808.08949.

Alec Radford, Karthik Narasimhan, Tim Salimans, and Ilya Sutskever. 2018. Improving Language Understanding by Generative Pre-Training. page 12.

Olga Russakovsky, Jia Deng, Hao Su, Jonathan Krause, Sanjeev Satheesh, Sean Ma, Zhiheng Huang, Andrej Karpathy, Aditya Khosla, Michael Bernstein, Alexander C. Berg, and Li Fei-Fei. 2014. ImageNet Large Scale Visual Recognition Challenge. *arXiv:1409.0575 [cs]*. ArXiv: 1409.0575.

Naomi Saphra and Adam Lopez. 2018. Understanding Learning Dynamics Of Language Models with SVCCA. *arXiv:1811.00225 [cs]*. ArXiv: 1811.00225.

Rico Sennrich, Barry Haddow, and Alexandra Birch. 2016. Neural Machine Translation of Rare Words with Subword Units. In *Proceedings of the 54th Annual Meeting of the Association for Computational Linguistics (Volume 1: Long Papers)*, pages 1715–1725, Berlin, Germany. Association for Computational Linguistics.

Xing Shi, Inkit Padhi, and Kevin Knight. 2016. Does String-Based Neural MT Learn Source Syntax? In *Proceedings of the 2016 Conference on Empirical Methods in Natural Language Processing*, pages 1526–1534, Austin, Texas. Association for Computational Linguistics.

Milan Straka and Jana Straková. 2017. Tokenizing, pos tagging, lemmatizing and parsing ud 2.0 with udpipe. In *Proceedings of the CoNLL 2017 Shared Task: Multilingual Parsing from Raw Text to Universal Dependencies*, pages 88–99, Vancouver, Canada. Association for Computational Linguistics.

Wilson L Taylor. 1953. cloze procedure: A new tool for measuring readability. *Journalism Bulletin*, 30(4):415–433.

Ian Tenney, Dipanjan Das, and Ellie Pavlick. 2019. Bert rediscovers the classical nlp pipeline. *arXiv preprint arXiv:1905.05950*.

Ian Tenney, Patrick Xia, Berlin Chen, Alex Wang, Adam Poliak, R. Thomas McCoy, Najoung Kim, Benjamin Van Durme, Samuel R. Bowman, Dipanjan Das, and Ellie Pavlick. 2018. What do you learn from context? Probing for sentence structure in contextualized word representations.

Ashish Vaswani, Noam Shazeer, Niki Parmar, Jakob Uszkoreit, Llion Jones, Aidan N. Gomez, Lukasz Kaiser, and Illia Polosukhin. 2017. Attention Is All You Need. *arXiv:1706.03762 [cs]*. ArXiv: 1706.03762.

Adina Williams, Nikita Nangia, and Samuel Bowman. 2018. A Broad-Coverage Challenge Corpus for Sentence Understanding through Inference. In *Proceedings of the 2018 Conference of the North American Chapter of the Association for Computational Linguistics: Human Language Technologies, Volume 1 (Long Papers)*, pages 1112–1122, New Orleans, Louisiana. Association for Computational Linguistics.

Daniel Zeman, Jan Hajič, Martin Popel, Martin Potthast, Milan Straka, Filip Ginter, Joakim Nivre, and Slav Petrov. 2018. Conll 2018 shared task: Multilingual parsing from raw text to universal dependencies. In *Proceedings of the CoNLL 2018 Shared Task: Multilingual Parsing from Raw Text to Universal Dependencies*, pages 1–21.

# Cross-Domain Sentiment Classification using Vector Embedded Domain Representations

**Nicolaj Filrup Rasmussen**
IT University of Copenhagen
nicr@itu.dk

**Kristian Nørgaard Jensen**
IT University of Copenhagen
krnj@itu.dk

**Marco Placenti**
IT University of Copenhagen
mapl@itu.dk

**Thai Wang**
IT University of Copenhagen
twan@itu.dk

## Abstract

Due to the differences between reviews in different product categories, creating a general model for cross-domain sentiment classification can be a difficult task. This paper proposes an architecture that incorporates domain knowledge into a neural sentiment classification model. In addition to providing a cross-domain model, this also provides a quantifiable representation of the domains as numeric vectors. We show that it is possible to cluster the domain vectors and provide qualitative insights into the inter-domain relations. We also a) present a new data set for sentiment classification that includes a domain parameter and preprocessed data points, and b) perform an ablation study in order to determine whether some word groups impact performance.

## 1 Introduction

In recent years the amount of text data has been growing exponentially. With the growth of social media and the success of e-commerce, large websites such as Amazon have developed great interest in online user reviews, which the users are able to write about every product. The task of classifying review sentiments poses little challenge for humans. However, with large amount of data comes the necessity of automating such tedious classification tasks, which proves to be a challenge that needs careful development and consideration.

This challenge arises because reviewers use different registers when writing reviews across product domains. Consequently, machines are not well equipped to catch those differences. The differences are easy to detect when users reference domain-specific words or other products in the same category. This belongs to a domain-specific knowledge that a neural network needs to learn in order to fully understand the differences and the similarities within the context of the reviews. Thus, for a classifier to perform well at this task, it may be important to include a way for it to represent these domains.

In this paper, we propose a novel, yet effective way of representing domains in sentiment classification. Using this representation we will show that it is possible to visualize relations between domains. This will allow clustering of similar product categories in the feature space of the domain representations. We also attempt to evaluate whether these groupings are similar to those made by humans.

Implementing the domain representations as a vector embedding provides a simple and elegant solution compared to previous solutions like Peng et al. (2018) and Liu et al. (2018). The aim of this paper is to develop a cross-domain sentiment classification model achieving comparable performance to those of existing methods, with the added benefit of insights into the inter-domain relations. Additionally we have developed a small but interesting data set building on top of McAuley et al. (2015). Our main contribution being balancing and preprocessing the data, as well as adding the domain in an easy to parse way. The data set is available at https://static.nfz.dk/data.zip.

## 2 Related Work

Sentiment classification is a well-established and -researched field within natural language processing. Pang et al. (2002) tested three machine learning algorithms for performing sentiment classification on sampled movie review data. Go et al. (2009) also tested three machine learning algorithms. However, they wanted to test the performance on documents that include emoticons which are sampled from Twitter data.

Including domain knowledge in models is nothing new either. Alumäe (2013) has used domain information to train a language model that responds differently in different domains. Tilk and Alumäe (2014) presented a Recurrent Neural Language model used for training an Automatic Speech Recognition system. Ammar et al. (2016) presented a multilingual model for parsing sentences, in which languages are encoded in their own variable.

Peng et al. (2018) presented a method for performing cross-domain sentiment classification on sparse labeled domains using domain adaption. The paper proposes a co-learned model which uses target specific features and domain invariant features to classify sentiment. Performing multi-domain classification has received little attention within Natural Language Processing. Nam and Han (2016) used multi-domain classification for visual tracking. More recently Jia et al. (2019) performed cross-domain NER by using a parameter generation network to learn domain and task correlations. They did this in an unsupervised setting and achieved state-of-the-art results among the supervised counterparts.

Li and Zong (2008) proposed two different ways of performing multi-domain sentiment classification. One was combining the domains at the feature level and the other was combining it at the classifier level. When combining at the classifier level, one could also think of using a multiple classifier system (MCS). Li et al. (2011) proposed using an MCS for performing multi-domain sentiment classification. Here they applied both fixed and trained rules for combining the output of the classifiers. Liu et al. (2018) proposed that multi-domain sentiment classification can be done for both abundant and sparse labeled domains, using domain specific representations. They produced domain general representations using a Bi-LSTM and learning domain descriptors using an attention network. Moreover, they trained a separate domain classifier using the domain general representations. The whole model was trained using a minimax game.

The model proposed in this paper uses a structure similar to the latter but distinguishes itself by being simpler, allowing for faster training or training on more modest hardware. The proposed architecture excludes the domain classifier and approaches the task of learning domain specific features using vector embeddings. In addition, great emphasis is put on the embedded vectors produced during training and what they can tell us about the relations of the domains.

## 3 Methodology

The proposed model is composed of three blocks, as shown in Figure 1.

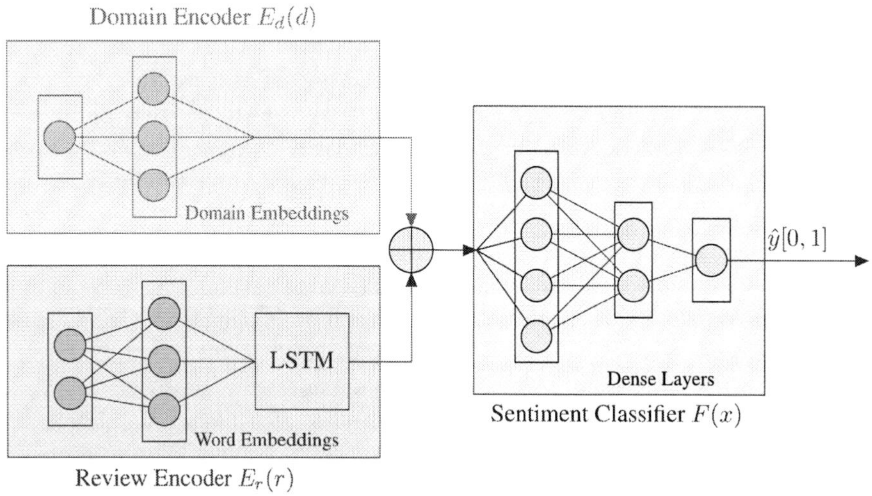


Figure 1: Our proposed model architecture

- Domain encoder $E_d(d)$
- Review encoder $E_r(r)$
- Sentiment classifier $F(x)$

Two of the blocks, $E_d(d)$ and $E_r(r)$, work as encoders, encoding the incoming data and making it usable for the final classifier. The classifier is a simple feed forward neural network that uses the encoded data to classify the review as either positive or negative. The blocks are described in more details in Sections 3.2 to 3.4.

### 3.1 Data set generation

The data used in this paper has been collected from Amazon (McAuley et al., 2015). All of the collected reviews are in English.

12 domains were selected and 200,000 reviews were sampled from each (100,000 positives and 100,000 negatives). The reviews were sampled at random. In total, 2.4 million reviews were collected from the 12 domains (See Table 1). The data set is structured such that each data point consists of the following four attributes: $y$, $review$, $topic$, $length$. Here $y$ corresponds to the correct sentiment label, $review$ is the tokenized review which is also segmented into sentences, $topic$ is the domain label and $length$ denotes the number of sentences in the review.

| Category | Negative | Positive | Total |
|---|---|---|---|
| Automotive | 100K | 100K | 200K |
| Baby | 100K | 100K | 200K |
| Beauty | 100K | 100K | 200K |
| CD's and Vinyl | 100K | 100K | 200K |
| Cell Phones | 100K | 100K | 200K |
| Electronics | 100K | 100K | 200K |
| Personal Care | 100K | 100K | 200K |
| Movies and TV | 100K | 100K | 200K |
| Office Products | 100K | 100K | 200K |
| Sports | 100K | 100K | 200K |
| Toys and Games | 100K | 100K | 200K |
| Video Games | 100K | 100K | 200K |

Table 1: List of domains sampled from (McAuley et al., 2015)

First and foremost, we concatenate each review text onto its summary text, effectively treating the summary text as the first sentence. This is done to use all of the data available.

When the review and summary have been concatenated, we segment the text into sentences using a sentence segmenter from NLTK.[1] The segmenter is trained on the full data set in order to fit the style and abbreviations used in the reviews. This enables identification of a part-of-speech (POS) tag for each word using a pre-trained POS tagger. The POS tagger is from NLTK and uses the Penn Treebank tagset. Using these tags it is possible to create new data sets with certain word groups ablated. Each sentence is subsequently tokenized into words with the exception of digits and some punctuation.[2] The sentence split is not used in this model but is available in the data set for future research.

| Data set | Unique tokens |
|---|---|
| Full data set | 27,112 |
| Ablated adjectives | 24,225 |
| Ablated stop words | 26,962 |

Table 2: Vocab sizes of the constructed data sets

Lastly, we choose to only include words that occur more than 100 times in the vocabulary and represent the discarded tokens with an <UNK> token. This is done purely to limit the size of the vocabulary. The vocabulary size for each of the three data sets can be seen in Table 2. The three vocabularies mentioned here are the full set with all word groups: the set where adjectives have been removed and the set where stop words have been removed. The stop word list used is from NLTK.

### 3.2 Domain Encoder

The Domain Encoder takes one of the 12 domains presented in Table 1 and encodes it into its own internal representation. The idea behind this architecture is to make the model learn its own representations for each domain (Mikolov et al., 2013) and how they relate to each other. There are several ways of implementing this representation, but the choice to use vector embeddings was made because it is simple and because they are easy to interpret compared to some of the more abstract methods of representation. Each domain is represented by a 50-dimensional vector that is learned during training. A 50-dimensional vector is chosen to match the size of the pre-trained word vectors in the Review Encoder (Section 3.3). The domain representations are randomly initialized using a uniform distribution.

### 3.3 Review Encoder

This encoder takes a vector of variable length for the input layer, meaning that the layer adapts itself continuously according to the sentence given as input. We set a threshold to 500 tokens, effectively truncating sequences longer than this. Each token in the sequence is represented by pre-trained GloVe embeddings (Pennington et al., 2014). The output of the Review Encoder is an LSTM layer with 64 neurons (Hochreiter and Schmidhuber, 1997).

### 3.4 Sentiment Classifier

The two previous outputs (from the Domain Encoder and the Review Encoder) are concatenated together, resulting in a vector of length 114 as input for the Sentiment Classifier. The Sentiment Classifier is a standard feed forward neural network, where the first hidden layer consists of 128 neurons, which is followed by a second hidden layer consisting of 64 neurons. Finally, we have a single neuron which outputs the probability of the sentence being positive. The probability is rounded to the nearest integer, where 1 is considered positive and 0 is negative.

[1] http://www.nltk.org

[2] Included punctuation: ... : ; , ( ) ! ? " '

### 3.5 Hyper Parameters

The model's hyper parameters are tuned using random search. The implementation is provided by an open source project (Autonomio, 2019).

The data set used for the hyper parameter tuning consists of 150,000 samples, which were sampled from the full training set. From this, 50,000 samples are sampled for validation and the remaining 100,000 samples are used for training. This split is performed 5 times resulting in 5 different validation/train splits. When sampling we make sure the resulting data sets are balanced between the sentiment labels. For each run, one of the splits is selected at random in order not to fit to a specific data set. We evaluate each set of parameters based on the accuracy score achieved by the model on the sampled validation set.

### 3.6 Experiments

We analyze the relevance that the domain embedding has in our model by testing our model twice, once with the Domain Encoder and once without. These two experiments are run 4 times and the mean is reported. Furthermore, we test the proposed architecture by ablating adjectives and stop words separately. In total we conduct 4 different experiments on the model. We split the data set such that we have around 2 million reviews for training, 200,000 for validation and 200,000 as a hidden test set. In all four cases we run 10 epochs of training while validating in between epochs. Finally, we evaluate on the hidden test set.

The experiments are executed on a machine with an NVIDIA Tesla T4 GPU, 8 CPUs, 16GB of RAM, Keras 2.2.4 and TensorFlow 1.13.1.

## 4 Results

In this section the results of our experiments will be presented.

### 4.1 Domain Encoder

In this section, we will outline the performance of the model with and without the domain encoder.

| Model | Accuracy | Recall | Precision | F1 |
|---|---|---|---|---|
| W/ domains | 0.8910 | 0.8914 | 0.8992 | 0.8953 |
| W/o domains | 0.8929 | 0.9143 | 0.8752 | 0.8943 |

Table 3: Model performance with and without the domain encoder

The performance impact of the domain encoder is outlined in Table 3. The results in the table are mean accuracy, recall, precision and F1 for 4 runs of 10 epochs for both configurations. As can be seen, the inclusion of the domain encoder does not seem to significantly impact performance, with the exception of slightly slower convergence as visualized in Figure 2. The shaded areas around the curves denote mean $\pm$ 1 standard deviation.

The model with the domain encoder has a smoother learning curve (fewer jumps) during the first couple of epochs. The spike in standard deviation around epoch 5 is caused by a single outlier run.

The accuracy and recall with the domain encoder are slightly worse, whereas the precision is slightly improved. Moreover, when looking at the F1 score we see a slight favor for using the domain encoder. This, in combination with the small differences, makes it hard to determine if performance is impacted either way. This will be discussed further in section 5.

### 4.2 Ablation Studies

During our research, we wanted to study the impact of ablating certain features of the re-

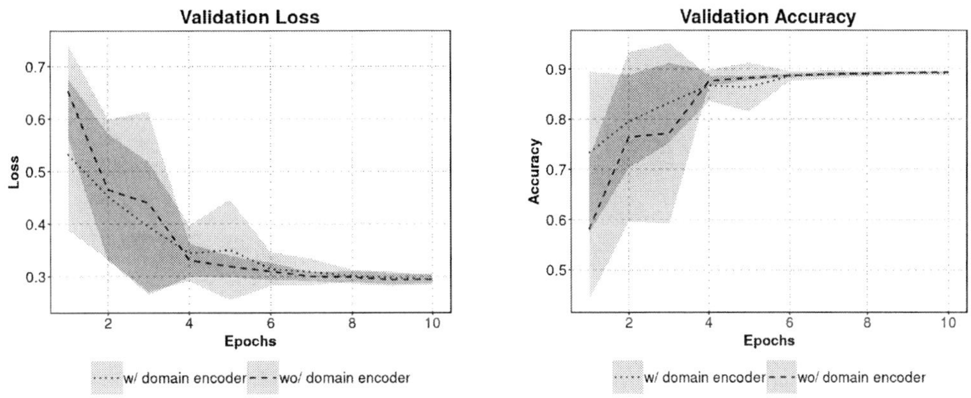


(a) The mean loss learning curves for the two configurations of the model

(b) The mean accuracy learning curves for the two configurations of the model

Figure 2: Loss and accuracy of the model with and without the domain encoder

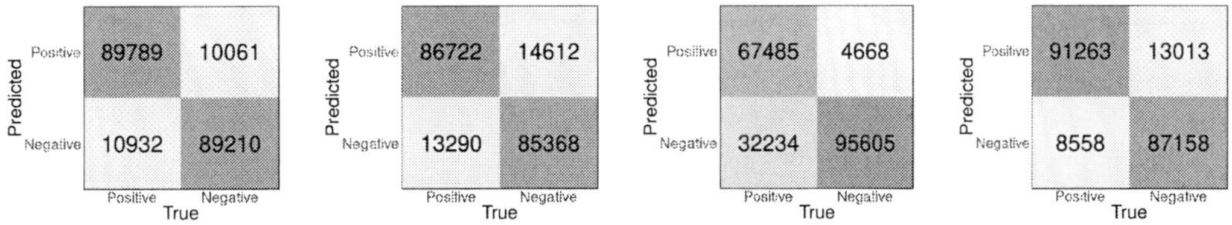


(a) Using all features

(b) Ablating adjectives

(c) Ablating stop words

(d) Ablating domains

Figure 3: Confusion matrices

view data. We wanted to do this to understand which word groups are particularly important for performing sentiment classification across multiple domains.

We hypothesized that adjectives and stop words were two important feature groups for determining sentiment and thus performed an ablation study on these.

The hypothesis for the stop words was based on the knowledge that the list of stop words used contains many negations such as 'not', which will distort the data. The reason for choosing adjectives was that certain descriptors of products might be negative or positive and that we may therefore see an impact in performance once those have been removed.

The domain encoder is included during the ablation experiments. The performance of a model in each of the studies plus a baseline, which is a model using all features of the data, can be found in tabular form in Table 4. These performance metrics are calculated on an unseen test set after training each model. For comparison the model without domain encoder is included as well.

| Model | Loss | Accuracy |
|---|---|---|
| Using all features | 0.2940 | 0.8910 |
| Ablating stop words | 0.4015 | 0.8185 |
| Ablating adjectives | 0.3803 | 0.8605 |
| Without domain encoder | 0.2943 | 0.8929 |

Table 4: Final performance on hidden test set in ablation studies

To further investigate these results, confusion matrices have been produced. They can be seen in Figure 3.

### 4.3 Domain Representations

The learned domain representations are extracted from the model and reduced in dimensionality using the PCA algorithm. To interpret the similarities between the representations, we employ hierarchical clustering analysis using ward linkage. In Figure 4 the result of the clustering analysis is displayed in a dendrogram.

## 5 Discussion

In this section, the implications of Section 4 will be discussed.

### 5.1 Domain Encoder

As discussed in Section 4.1, the performance does not seem to be greatly impacted by the addition of the domain encoder. In this section, we will attempt to highlight a few interesting observations about the architecture that could be potential points of further research.

Table 5 shows that the difference in accuracy is small. The accuracy after adding the domain encoder is slightly worse for almost all classes, but there does not appear to be a large inter-class difference in performance impact.

In Figure 5, we see the standard deviation of accuracy during training. The lower this value, the more consistent the model performs across runs.

What we see here is that the model with the domain encoder has a lower standard deviation initially. This suggests that the model is more consistent. Here we can also study the impact of the outlier observed in Section 4.1. We see clearly that the outlier has a large impact and that the rest of the runs are much more in agreement.

| Domain | W/ domains | W/o domains |
|---|---|---|
| Automotive | 0.8945 | 0.8957 |
| Baby | 0.9140 | 0.9140 |
| Beauty | 0.9041 | 0.9046 |
| CD's and Vinyl | 0.8534 | 0.8564 |
| Cell Phones | 0.9053 | 0.9079 |
| Electronics | 0.9024 | 0.9051 |
| Personal Care | 0.8931 | 0.8940 |
| Movies and TV | 0.8602 | 0.8635 |
| Office Products | 0.9013 | 0.9029 |
| Sports | 0.8943 | 0.8969 |
| Toys and Games | 0.8945 | 0.8941 |
| Video Games | 0.8792 | 0.8816 |

Table 5: Per domain accuracy performance with and without the domain encoder

Based on these results it could be argued that stability is increased, but without ensuring that the outlier observed is as rare as we assume, this cannot be concluded with any certainty. In addition, this stability seems to be inconsequential in this case as convergence is reached around the same time anyway.

### 5.2 Ablation Studies

Since we are developing a new model, and subsequently a new data set, we want to investigate whether or not all features (word groups in this case) of the data are important for sentiment classification across domains. In the case of this research, we theorized that both stop words and adjectives would be important for the performance. The aim of this part of the study is to verify some assumptions about the data set.

As shown in Table 4, the feature with the largest impact on performance is stop words. Negations are part of our stop word list. Therefore the distinction between classes will become less obvious for a model to see. The confusion matrix in Figure 3c shows that when stop words are removed the model predicts that positive samples are negative. In

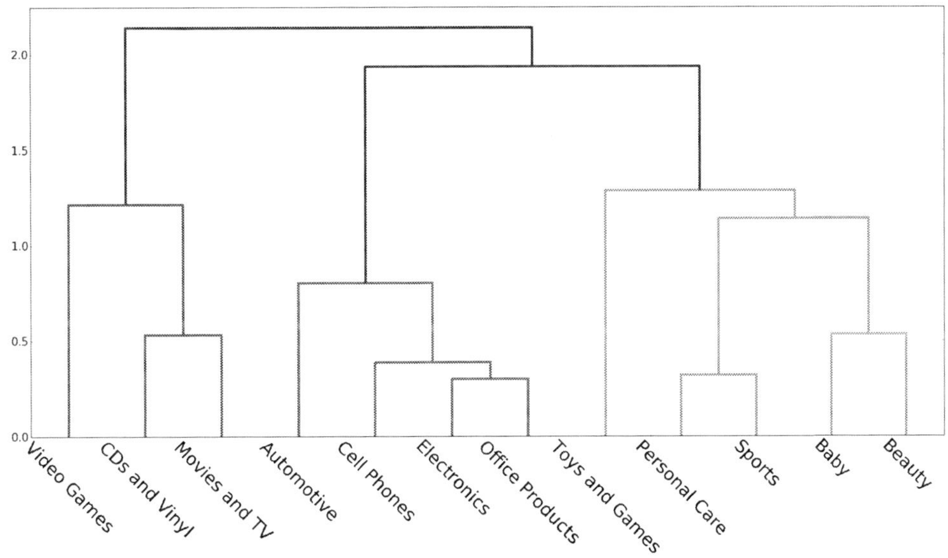


Figure 4: Dendrogram showing the clusters created by the HCA algorithm

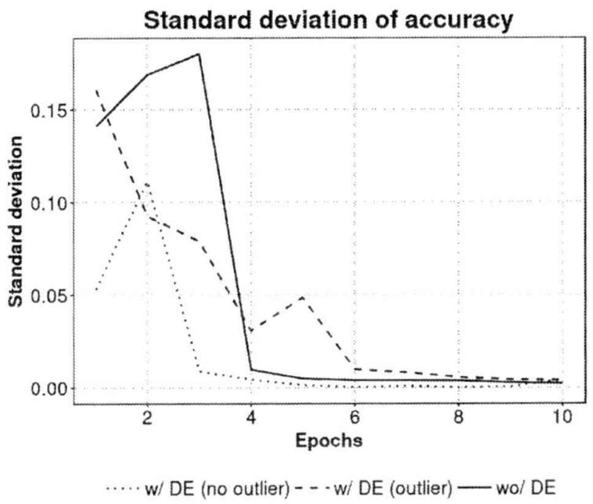


Figure 5: Standard deviation over time (DE = Domain Encoder)

fact, it predicts that 32% of all positive samples in the test set are negative. This is a major flaw with this model, as it predicts negative samples very well.

In Table 4, we see that ablating adjectives has less impact than ablating stop words. Also when looking at Figure 3b we see that ablating adjectives decreases overall performance thus not penalizing one class over the other.

These observations lead us to believe that our initial hypothesis of certain adjectives being used as a polarity marker, seems to not hold. However, the overall performance without adjectives is worse than with, so there might be some specific words that could be found during further research.

### 5.3 Domain Representations

As mentioned in Section 4.3, we use Hierarchical Cluster Analysis (HCA) to get insights into the similarities of the domain representations.

Doing this we get statistical insights into the similarities between the generated domain representations. These insights are presented in the dendrogram in Figure 4. The clustering provides us with three groups of domains that it finds the most similar. These three are the "green" (group 1), "red" (group 2) and "light blue" (group 3) groups.

Group 1 consists of digital media content domains: "Movies and TV", "CD's and Vinyls" and "Video Games". It seems reasonable from a human point of view that these domains would be closely related. However, as can be seen in Figure 4, "Video Games" is the most distant domain in Group 1, merging with the others late in the clustering process.

Group 2 consists mainly of consumer electronics, with the odd one out being cars. It makes sense that cars is the least close of the bunch, but with the recent trend of adding a lot of electronics to cars, it is certainly not unreasonable that automotive reviews would share a lot of language with consumer electronics. Moreover, a lot of accessories, such as phone holders and chargers, are sold in the automotive category, leading to higher similarity.

Group 3 is definitely the most diverse of the three, containing seemingly unrelated domains like "Beauty" and "Toys and Games". What the results suggest is that these categories may share some language characteristics at least in the context of determining the sentiment of the reviews. As we see though, the category of "Toys and Games" is less similar to any of the other domains within the group than the rest of the domains are to each other. However, it is more similar to the domains within its own group than to domains in other groups. We also see that the similarity between the two inner clusters of group 3 is small.

## 6 Conclusion

In the present work we have presented a model which represents domains as vectors and a way of understanding how the classifier is discriminating between different domains. The results seem to suggest that the model accurately captures the inter-domain relationships.

The model achieves performance comparable to that of a model without the proposed domain encoder, with hints at possible stability gains early in training.

Moreover, we find that stop words is an important feature group when performing sentiment classification. This is especially true when comparing to the importance of adjectives. While the performance does take a hit by removing the adjectives, it is not nearly as bad as with the stop words.

The convergence characteristics of the model would be an interesting point of further research. Moreover, looking into the use of the domain embeddings as a way of doing domain adaptation would also be a logical next step for this model.

## 7 Acknowledgement

We thank Barbara Plank for her guidance and advice. We would not have gotten this far without her.

## References


Tanel Alumäe. 2013. Multi-domain neural network language model. In *INTERSPEECH-2013*, pages 2182–2186.

Waleed Ammar, George Mulcaire, Miguel Ballesteros, Chris Dyer, and Noah A. Smith. 2016. Many languages, one parser. *Transactions of the Association for Computational Linguistics*, 4:431–444.

Autonomio. 2019. Talos. Retrieved from http://github.com/autonomio/talos.

Alec Go, Richa Bhayani, and Lei Huang. 2009. Twitter sentiment classification using distant supervision. *CS224N Project Report, Stanford*, 1(12):2009.

Sepp Hochreiter and Jürgen Schmidhuber. 1997. Long short-term memory. *Neural Comput.*, 9(8):1735–1780.

Chen Jia, Xiaobo Liang, and Yue Zhang. 2019. Cross-domain ner using cross-domain language modeling. In *Proceedings of the 57th Conference of the Association for Computational Linguistics*, pages 2464–2474.

Shou-Shan Li, Chu-Ren Huang, and Cheng-Qing Zong. 2011. Multi-domain sentiment classification with classifier combination. *Journal of Computer Science and Technology*, 26(1):25–33.

Shoushan Li and Chengqing Zong. 2008. Multi-domain sentiment classification. In *Proceedings of the 46th Annual Meeting of the Association for Computational Linguistics on Human Language Technologies: Short Papers*, HLT-Short '08, pages 257–260, Stroudsburg, PA, USA. Association for Computational Linguistics.

Qi Liu, Yue Zhang, and Jiangming Liu. 2018. Learning domain representation for multi-domain sentiment classification. *Proceedings of the 2018 Conference of the North American Chapter of the Association for Computational Linguistics: Human Language Technologies, Volume 1 (Long Papers)*.

Julian McAuley, Christopher Targett, Qinfeng Shi, and Anton Van Den Hengel. 2015. Image-based recommendations on styles and substitutes. In *Proceedings of the 38th International ACM SIGIR Conference on Research and Development in Information Retrieval*, pages 43–52. ACM.

Tomas Mikolov, Ilya Sutskever, Kai Chen, Greg S Corrado, and Jeff Dean. 2013. Distributed representations of words and phrases and their compositionality. In *Advances in neural information processing systems*, pages 3111–3119.

Hyeonseob Nam and Bohyung Han. 2016. Learning multi-domain convolutional neural networks for visual tracking. In *Proceedings of the IEEE conference on computer vision and pattern recognition*, pages 4293–4302.

Bo Pang, Lillian Lee, and Shivakumar Vaithyanathan. 2002. Thumbs up?: Sentiment classification using machine learning techniques. In *Proceedings of the ACL-02 Conference on Empirical Methods in Natural Language Processing - Volume 10*, EMNLP '02, pages 79–86, Stroudsburg, PA, USA. Association for Computational Linguistics.

Minlong Peng, Qi Zhang, Yu-gang Jiang, and Xuanjing Huang. 2018. Cross-domain sentiment classification with target domain specific information. In *Proceedings of the 56th Annual Meeting of the Association for Computational Linguistics (Volume 1: Long Papers)*, pages 2505–2513.

Jeffrey Pennington, Richard Socher, and Christopher Manning. 2014. Glove: Global vectors for word representation. In *Proceedings of the 2014 conference on empirical methods in natural language processing (EMNLP)*, pages 1532–1543.

Ottokar Tilk and Tanel Alumäe. 2014. Multi-domain neural network language model. In *Baltic HLT*, pages 149–152.

# Multiclass Text Classification on Unbalanced, Sparse and Noisy Data

**Tillmann Dönicke**[1], **Florian Lux**[2], and **Matthias Damaschk**[3]

University of Stuttgart
Institute for Natural Language Processing
Pfaffenwaldring 5 b
D-70569 Stuttgart
{doenictn[1], luxfn[2], damascms[3]}@ims.uni-stuttgart.de

## Abstract

This paper discusses methods to improve the performance of text classification on data that is difficult to classify due to a large number of unbalanced classes with noisy examples. A variety of features are tested, in combination with three different neural-network-based methods with increasing complexity. The classifiers are applied to a songtext–artist dataset which is large, unbalanced and noisy. We come to the conclusion that substantial improvement can be obtained by removing unbalancedness and sparsity from the data. This fulfils a classification task unsatisfactorily—however, with contemporary methods, it is a practical step towards fairly satisfactory results.

## 1 Introduction

Text classification tasks are omnipresent in natural language processing (NLP). Various classifiers may perform better or worse, depending on the data they are given (eg. Uysal and Gunal, 2014). However, there is data where one would expect to find a correlation between (vectorised) texts and classes, but the expectation is not met and the classifiers achieve poor results. One example for such data are songtexts with the corresponding artists being classes. A classification task on this data is especially hard due to multiple handicaps:

First, the number of classes is extraordinarily high (compared to usual text classification tasks). Second, the number of samples for a class varies between a handful and more than a hundred. And third, songtexts are structurally and stylistically more diverse than, e.g., newspaper texts, as they may be organised in blocks of choruses and verses, exhibit rhyme, make use of slang language etc. (cf. Mayer et al., 2008). In addition, we try to predict something latent, since there is no direct mapping between artists and their songtexts. A lot of the texts are not written by the singers themselves, but by professional songwriters (Smith et al., 2019, p. 5). Hence the correlation that a classifier should capture is between songtexts that the writers think to fit a specific artist and the artist. All these points make the task difficult; still, it is a task needed for nowadays' NLP systems, e.g., in a framework that suggests new artists to a listener based on the songtexts s/he likes. Thus, to tackle the challenges given is a helpful step for any task in the field of NLP that might come with similarly difficult data.

For the artist classification, we investigate three neural-network-based methods: a one-layer perceptron, a two-layer Doc2Vec model and a multi-layer perceptron. (A detailed description of the models shall follow in section 2.) Besides the model, the representation of the instances in a feature space is important for classification, thus we also aim to find expressive features for the particular domain of songtexts. (See section 4 for a list of our features.)[1]

## 2 Methods

The following sections shall provide an overview of our classifiers in order of increasing complexity.

### 2.1 Perceptron

A perceptron is a very simple type of neural network that was first described in Rosenblatt (1958). It contains only one layer, which is at the same time the input and output layer. The input is a feature vector $\vec{x}$ extracted from a data sample $x$. Every possible class $y \in Y$ is associated with a weight vector $\vec{w}_y$. A given sample $x$ is classified as $\hat{y}_x$ as follows:

[1]The code will be made available at https://github.com/ebaharilikult/DL4NLP.

$$\hat{y}_x = \underset{y \in Y}{\arg\max}\, \vec{x} \cdot \vec{w}_y \tag{1}$$

During training, every training sample is classified using the perceptron. If the classification is incorrect, the weights of the incorrectly predicted class are decreased, whereas the weights of the class that would have been correct are reinforced.

Additions to this basic system include shuffling of the training data, batch learning and a dynamic learning rate. The shuffling of the training data across multiple epochs shall prevent the order of the samples from having an effect on the learning process. Batch learning generally improves the performance of a perceptron (e.g. McDonald et al., 2010); hereby all updates are jointly performed after each epoch instead of each sample. This removes a strong preference for the last seen class if the information in the features of multiple samples overlaps greatly. A dynamic learning rate improves the convergence of the weights. It gives updates that happen later during training less impact and allows a closer approximation to optimal weights.

### 2.2 Doc2Vec

Doc2Vec (Le and Mikolov, 2014) is a two-layer neural network model which learns vector representations of documents, so-called paragraph vectors. It is an extension of Word2Vec (Mikolov et al., 2013) which learns vector representations of words. Thereby, context words, represented as concatenated one-hot vectors, serve as input and are used to predict one target word. After training, the weight matrix of the hidden layer becomes the word matrix, containing the well-known Word2Vec word embeddings.

The extension in Doc2Vec is that a unique document/paragraph id is appended to each input n-gram, as if it was a context word. Since paragraph ids have to be different from all words in the vocabulary, the weight matrix can be separated into the word matrix and the paragraph matrix, the latter containing document embeddings.[2]

In a document classification task, labels instead of paragraph ids are used. By doing so, the Doc2Vec model learns vectors of each label instead of each document. If one wants to predict the label of an unseen document, a vector representation for this document needs to be inferred first. Therefore, a new column/row is added to the paragraph matrix. Then the n-grams of the document are iteratively fed to the network (as in training). However, the word matrix as well as the weight matrix of the output layer are kept fixed, and so only the paragraph matrix is updated. The resulting paragraph vector for the unseen document is finally compared to the paragraph vectors representing labels; and the label of the most similar vector is returned as the prediction.

### 2.3 MLP

A multi-layer perceptron (Beale and Jackson, 1990), also referred to as feed forward neural network, is a deep neural network consisting of multiple hidden layers with neurons which are fully connected with the neurons of the next layer, and an output layer with as many neurons as classes. The number of layers and the number of neurons in each hidden layer depends on the classification tasks and are therefore hyperparameters. For multiclass classification, the softmax function is used in the output layer. During training, the backpropagation learning algorithm (Rumelhart et al., 1985) based on the gradient descent algorithm, updates the weights and reduces the error of the chosen cost function, such as mean squared error or cross-entropy.

To prevent overfitting in neural networks, dropout (Srivastava et al., 2014) is commonly used. It omits hidden neurons with a certain probability to generalise more during training and thus enhances the model.[3]

## 3 Data

We use a dataset of 57,647 English songtexts with their corresponding artist and title, which has been downloaded from Kaggle[4]. The data was shuffled uniformly and 10% were held out for validation and test set, respectively.

There are 643 unique artists in the data. Table 1 shows the distribution of artists and songtexts for

[2] The described version of Word2Vec and Doc2Vec is commonly referred to as "continuous bag of words" (DBOW) model. If the input and output are swapped, i.e. a single word (Word2Vec) or document (Doc2Vec) is used to predict several context words, the architecture is called "skip-gram" (SG) or "distributed memory" (DM) model, respectively.

[3] It should be noted here that advanced deep learning models such as CNNs and RNNs exist and have been successfully used in text classification tasks (Lee and Dernoncourt, 2016), but have not been used in the context of this work and are therefore not explained in detail.

[4] `https://www.kaggle.com/mousehead/songlyrics`

| Dataset | Artists | Songs | Avg. songs |
|---|---|---|---|
| Training | 642 | 46,120 | 71.8 (44.0) |
| Validation | 612 | 5,765 | 9.4 (5.7) |
| Test | 618 | 5,765 | 9.3 (6.0) |

Table 1: Number of unique artists (classes), number of songtexts and average number of songtexts per artist (standard deviation in parentheses) for each dataset.

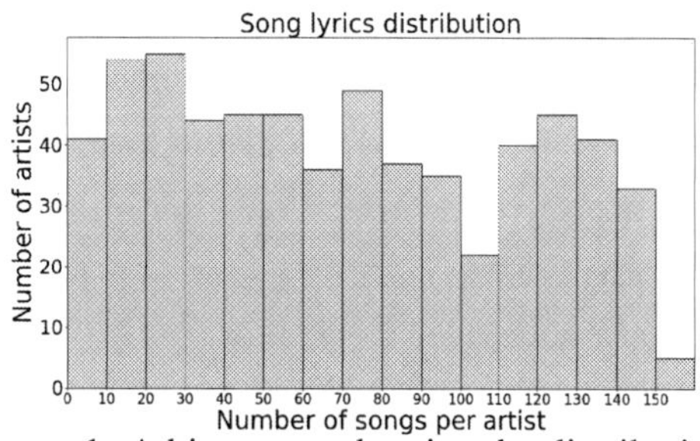


Figure 1: A histogram showing the distribution of songtexts in the training set.

each subset. The training set contains most of the unique artists (642) whereas less artists appear in the validation (612) and test set (618). Also, the standard deviation of average songs per artists is relatively high (i.e. more than half the average) which indicates that the number of songs per artists is spread over a large range.

The distribution of songs per artists in the training set can be seen in Figure 1. It shows similar counts for classes (artists) with many and classes with only a few samples (songtexts), i.e. unbalanced training data. The bandwidth goes from one artist with 159 songs to four artists with only one song which also illustrates the sparsity for some classes.

Besides the issues caused by the distribution of songtexts per artist, the quality of the texts is less than perfect. Nonsense words and sequences, such as *tu ru tu tu tu tu*, as well as spelling variations, such as *Yeaaah*, *Hey-A-Hey* and *aaaaaaalll-lllright!*, are very common.

## 4 Feature Extraction

For both the (single-layer) perceptron and the multi-layer perceptron we use the same preprocessing and features which are described below. (The Doc2Vec model uses its own integrated tokeniser and Word2Vec-based features.)

The songtexts are tokenised by whitespace. Within a token, all non-initial letters are lowercased and sequences of repeating letters are shortened to a maximum of three. To further reduce noise, punctuation is removed. The texts are tagged with parts-of-speech (POS) using the Apache OpenNLP maximum entropy tagger[5].

**Stylometric features** Generic information about the text, i.e. the number of lines, the number of tokens, the number of tokens that appear only once, the number of types and the average number of tokens per line.

**Rhyme feature** Number of unique line endings (in terms of the last two letters), normalised by the number of lines. This should serve as a simple measure for how well the lines rhyme.

**Word count vectors** Every unique word in the training corpus is assigned a unique dimension. In each dimension, the number of occurrences of the word in the sample are denoted. Term-frequency (tf) weighting is implemented, but can be switched on and off. As a minimal variant, only nouns can be taken into account; in this case we speak of noun count vectors.

**POS count vectors** The same as word count vectors after replacing all words with their POS tag.

**Word2Vec embeddings** 300-dimensional embeddings created from the Google news corpus.[6] The embedding of a text is hereby defined as the average of the embeddings of all the words in the text. As a minimal variant, only nouns can be taken into account.

**Bias** A feature with a constant value of 1 (to avoid zero vectors as feature vectors).

## 5 Experiments

This section lists the concrete parameter settings of the methods described in section 2. Since our models can only predict classes which have been encountered during training, only the 612 artists occurring in all subsets are kept for all evaluations. For another series of experiments, only the 40 unique artists with more songs than 140 in the training set are kept to reduce the impact of unbalancedness and sparsity (numbers in Table 2).

[5] `https://opennlp.apache.org/docs/1.8.0/manual/opennlp.html\#tools.postagger`

[6] GoogleNews-vectors-negative300.bin.gz from `https://code.google.com/archive/p/word2vec/`

| Dataset | Artists | Songs | Avg. songs |
|---|---|---|---|
| Training | 40 | 5,847 | 146.2 (4.6) |
| Validation | 40 | 646 | 16.2 (3.6) |
| Test | 40 | 714 | 17.9 (5.0) |

Table 2: Number of unique artists (classes), number of songtexts and average number of songtexts per artist (standard deviation in parentheses) for each dataset, keeping only the 40 unique artists with more songs than 140 in the training set.

### 5.1 Experimental Settings

**Perceptron** We train and test two versions of the perceptron. The minimal version (Perceptron) only uses noun count vectors without tf-weighting and the bias. The maximal version (Perceptron+) uses all features. All add-ons described in section 2.1 (shuffling, batch learning, dynamic learning rate) are used for both versions since they led to an increasing performance on the validation set in preliminary tests. For the decay of the learning rate, a linear decrease starting from 1 and ending at $\frac{1}{\text{number of epochs}}$ is chosen.

**Doc2Vec** For the Doc2Vec implementation, we use deeplearning4j[7] version 0.9. The hyperparamters are a minimum word frequency of 10, a hidden layer size of 300, a maximum window size of 8, and a learning rate starting at 0.025 and decreasing to 0.001. Tokenisation is performed by the incorporated UIMA tokeniser. The model is trained for 100 epochs with batch learning.[8]

**MLP** The implementation of MLP and MLP+ is done with Keras (Chollet et al., 2015). MLP+ uses all feature groups from section 4 and one bias feature for every group. The MLP+ model is shown in Figure 2. Each feature group uses multiple stacked layers that are then merged with a concatenation layer. The sizes of the dense layers are manually selected by trial and error. Several dropout layers with a constant probability of 0.2 are included. In contrast, MLP uses only the noun count vectors (as Perceptron) and thus only one input branch.

For both models, Adadelta, an optimisation function with adaptive learning rate, a batch size of 32 and categorical cross-entropy as the loss function are used. For the activation functions, rectified linear units are used in the hidden layer and softmax in the output layer. The model trains for 250 epochs and stores the weights that led to the best accuracy on the validation set through a checkpoint mechanism.

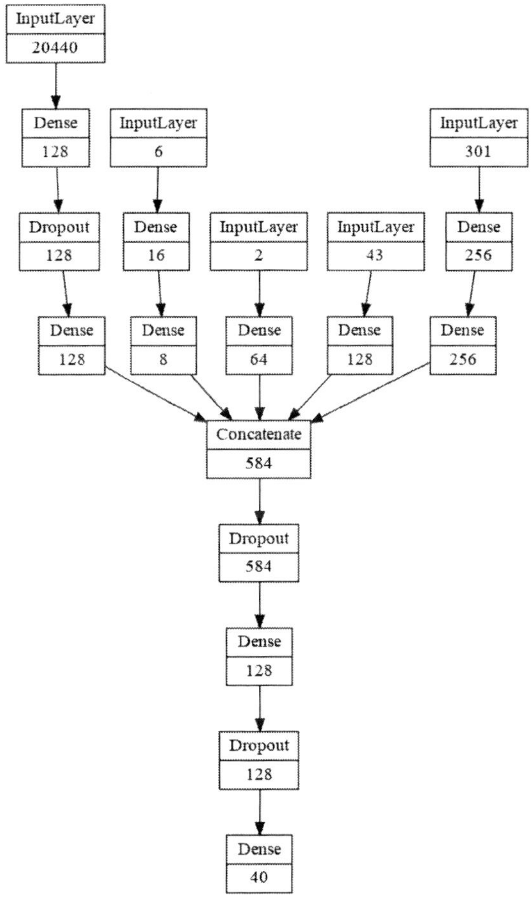


Figure 2: Model of the MLP+ model: Layers with corresponding number of neurons. The input layers correspond to the following feature groups (f.l.t.r.): word count vectors, stylometric features, rhyme feature, POS count vectors, Word2Vec embeddings.

### 5.2 Evaluation measures

Given a (test) set $X$, each sample $x \in X$ has a class $y_x$ and a prediction $\hat{y}_x$. Based on the predictions, we can calculate class-wise precision ($P$), recall ($R$) and $F$-score as follows:

$$P(y) = \frac{|\{x \in X \mid y_x = y \wedge y_x = \hat{y}_x\}|}{|\{x \in X \mid \hat{y}_x = y\}|} \quad (2)$$

[7] See https://deeplearning4j.org/docs/latest/deeplearning4j-nlp-doc2vec for a quick example.

[8] Since deeplearning4j does not document the possibility to get intermediate evaluation results during training, 10 models are trained separately for 10, 20, 30 etc. epochs to obtain data points for the learning progress analysis.

$$R(y) = \frac{|\{x \in X \mid y_x = y \wedge y_x = \hat{y}_x\}|}{|\{x \in X \mid y_x = y\}|} \quad (3)$$

$$F(y) = \frac{2 \cdot P(y) \cdot R(y)}{P(y) + R(y)} \quad (4)$$

The macro-averaged $F$-score of all classes is the average of the class-wise $F$-scores:

$$F_{macro} = \frac{1}{|Y|} \cdot \sum_{y \in Y} F(y) \quad (5)$$

For the overall precision and recall, the nominators and denominators are summed up for all $y \in Y$, resulting in:

$$P = R = \frac{|\{x \in X \mid y_x = \hat{y}_x\}|}{|\{x \in X\}|} \quad (6)$$

And the formula for the micro-averaged $F$-score:

$$F_{micro} = \frac{2 \cdot P \cdot R}{P + R} = P = R \quad (7)$$

The identity of overall $P$ and $R$ causes their identity with $F_{micro}$. This measure is identical with the overall accuracy (correct predictions divided by all predictions). Since $F_{macro}$ gives every class the same weight, but we deal with an unbalanced dataset, we choose $F_{micro}$ as evaluation measure and only show $F_{macro}$ in some graphs for comparison.

### 5.3 Results

Table 3 shows the micro-averaged $F$-score for all models. MLP+ performs best, followed by Perceptron and Doc2Vec. The use of additional features significantly decreases the performance of the perceptron (Perceptron+), but increases it for the multi-layer network (MLP+). This observation is discussed in section 5.4.

Figures 3–5 show the performance of Perceptron, Doc2Vec and MLP+ in dependence of the number of training epochs. The Perceptron (Figure 4) shows a generally increasing learning curve, i.e. more epochs lead to better results. Peaks like the one after the 51st epoch are ignored since the model uses a fixed number of 100 training epochs. Doc2Vec (Figure 5) reaches its best performance with 20 epochs and does not show any learning progress after that, even if trained for 100 epochs. The MLP+ model (Figure 3) exhibits increasing performance until around 100 training epochs and

| Model | MST | final | | best | |
|---|---|---|---|---|---|
| | | $F$ | ep. | $F$ | ep. |
| Perceptron | 0 | .066 | 100 | .069 | 94 |
| Perceptron+ | 0 | .003 | 100 | .006 | 23 |
| Doc2Vec | 0 | .032 | 100 | .033 | 70 |
| MLP | 0 | .023 | 97 | .025 | 114 |
| MLP+ | 0 | **.079** | 97 | .089 | 80 |
| Perceptron | 140 | .146 | 100 | .160 | 51 |
| Perceptron+ | 140 | .021 | 100 | .055 | 54 |
| Doc2Vec | 140 | .101 | 100 | .120 | 20 |
| MLP | 140 | .050 | 201 | .088 | 46 |
| MLP+ | 140 | **.182** | 105 | .193 | 109 |

Table 3: Micro-averaged $F$-score for each model on the test set after training (final) and during training (best), together with the corresponding training epochs. Lower part: only artists with more songs than (MST) 140 are kept in the training and the test set.

then reaches a plateau. Since the model uses that number of epochs which works best on the validation set (i.e. 105), it misses the best performance at the 109th epoch but gets a final score close to it.

### 5.4 Error Analysis

In this section, we shall focus on the confusion matrices produced by our three main models which are depicted in Figure 6 and to be read as follows: The x-axis and the y-axis represent artists in the same order (labels are omitted due to legibility). Each cell indicates how often the artist on the x-axis was classified as the artist on the y-axis (darker colours are higher numbers). The cells on the main diagonal correspond to the cases where a class was classified correctly hence a visible diagonal correlates with good results. Darker cells outside of the diagonal are significant misclassifications[9] and might be interesting to look into.

As is clearly visible in Figure 6 (a), something is wrong with the predictions of the Doc2Vec model. There are hints of a diagonal showing at the top-left—however, there are entire columns of dark colour. This means that there are classes that are almost always predicted, no matter which class a sample actually belongs to. Interestingly, we ob-

[9] Such mis-classifications will be denoted as outliers in the following, since we are talking about the correlation of the axes here.

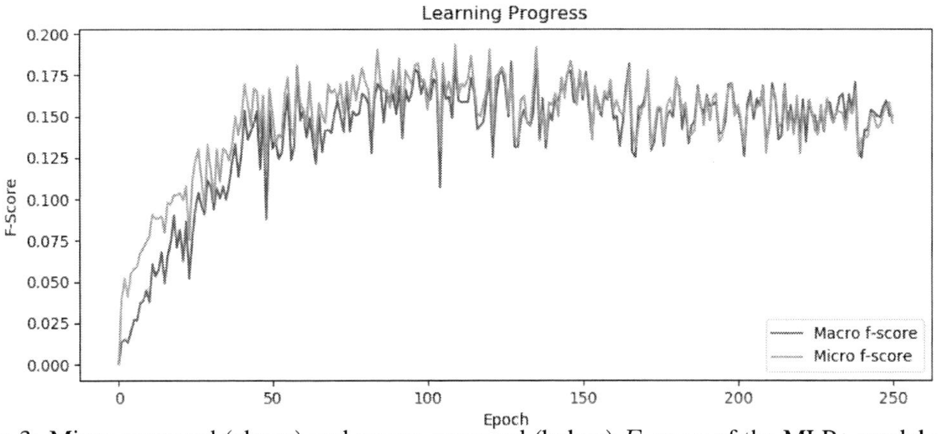


Figure 3: Micro-averaged (above) and macro-averaged (below) $F$-score of the MLP+ model on the test set (MST=140) after each training epoch.

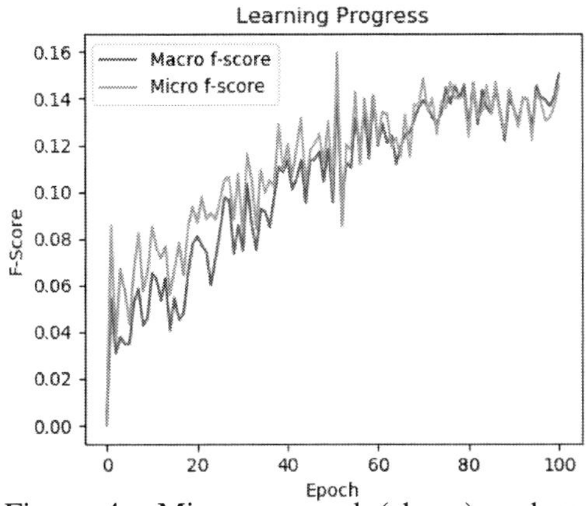


Figure 4: Micro-averaged (above) and macro-averaged (below) $F$-score of the Perceptron model on the test set (MST=140) after each training epoch.

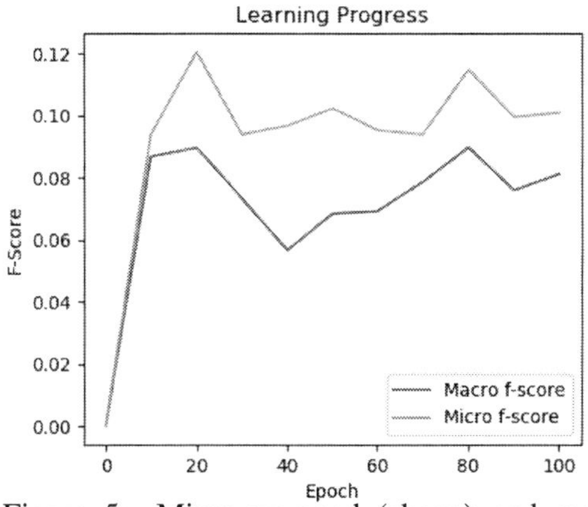


Figure 5: Micro-averaged (above) and macro-averaged (below) $F$-score of the Doc2Vec model on the test set (MST=140) for different numbers of training epochs.

served the same behaviour with our perceptron implementation in preliminary tests which changed when we started using batch learning. However, our Doc2Vec implementation already uses batch learning and mini-batch learning did not improve the performance in postliminary tests.

Figure 6 (b) shows that the perceptron performs well on most classes. However, there are very few classes where it actually recognises (almost) all of the samples. There are three major outliers and many outliers overall. This explains the rather low scores the model achieves, even though the diagonal is clearly visible. Looking at the three big outliers and engineering new features specifically for those could improve the performance. However, the informativeness of features can behave differently from what one might expect. Additional stylometric features that were specifically designed for the task lead to significantly worse results than the simple noun count vectors (Perceptron+ vs. Perceptron). However, this does not tell anything about the perceptron's performance when using other feature combinations.

The error distribution of the multi-layer perceptron is displayed in Figure 6 (c). Compared to the perceptron, most of the classes are predicted much better and there are less outliers overall. However, there are more major outliers which explains the still rather low performance. In further contrast to the perceptron, the use of all features leads to a performance increase (MLP+ vs. MLP). This is probably the case because the multi-layer percep-

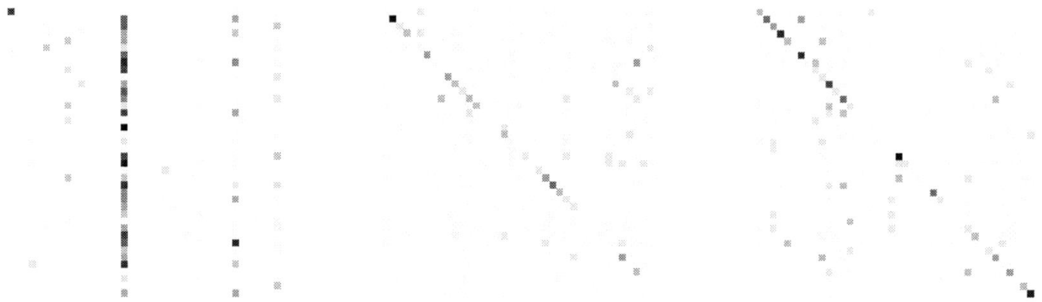

(a) Doc2Vec (b) Perceptron (c) MLP+

Figure 6: Confusion matrices of different models on the test set (MST=140).

tron can learn individual weights for the different feature groups through multiple branches and layers much better than the single-layer perceptron.

## 6 Summary & Conclusion

Songtext–artist classification is an example of multiclass text classification on unbalanced, sparse and noisy data. Three neural network models have been investigated on this specific task. 1) A single-layer perceptron which can be used for all kinds of classification on vectorised data. 2) Doc2Vec which is a contemporary tool for text classification. And 3) an extended multi-layer perceptron which we designed specifically for this task. While the third and most complex model achieves the best results, it becomes also visible that the choice of features has a significant effect on the classification performance. Here, too, the multi-layer network with its advanced combination of different, stylometric as well as count/ embedding-based, feature groups outperforms the other models.

We come to the conclusion that a vast number of and unbalanced classes as well as sparse and not directly correlated data do not allow for a perfect performance. Thus, given a text classification task where the data is as difficult, it makes sense to reduce the data to something that is manageable and meaningful. Sparse classes in a noisy sample space are little more than guesswork which might confuse the classifier and decrease the performance on more important classes. While it is somewhat obvious that removing difficult cases from the data improves the overall results, it is not something that one would usually do in a real-world application. We argue, that it can be a practical step to approach such a classification task, for elaborating the complexity of the classifier and engineering good features.

## 7 Future Work

A general clustering-based topic model encoded in new features could potentially improve the performance of songtext classifiers. Looking at our multi-layer perceptron, new features seem to be a good way to handle such difficult data. Other network architectures such as CNNs and RNNs can be considered worth a look as well since they improved (noisy) text classification in previous studies (e.g. Lai et al., 2015; Apostolova and Kreek, 2018).

Another way of dealing with imbalanced data is to apply oversampling to raise the number of samples for sparse classes, or undersampling to reduce the number of samples for frequent classes.

## 8 Acknowledgements

We thank the three anonymous reviewers for their valuable comments. This work emerged from a course at the Institute for Natural Language Processing of the University of Stuttgart; we thank our supervisors Evgeny Kim and Roman Klinger. We further thank Sebastian Padó for the organisational support.

## References

Emilia Apostolova and R. Andrew Kreek. 2018. Training and prediction data discrepancies: Challenges of text classification with noisy, historical data. *arXiv preprint arXiv:1809.04019*.

Russell Beale and Tom Jackson. 1990. *Neural Computing: An Introduction*, pages 67–73. CRC Press.

François Chollet et al. 2015. Keras: Deep learning library for theano and tensorflow. *URL: https://keras.io/k*, 7(8):T1.

Siwei Lai, Liheng Xu, Kang Liu, and Jun Zhao. 2015. Recurrent convolutional neural networks for text classification. In *Twenty-ninth AAAI conference on artificial intelligence*.

Quoc Le and Tomas Mikolov. 2014. Distributed representations of sentences and documents. In *International conference on machine learning*, pages 1188–1196.

Ji Young Lee and Franck Dernoncourt. 2016. Sequential short-text classification with recurrent and convolutional neural networks. *arXiv preprint arXiv:1603.03827*.

Rudolf Mayer, Robert Neumayer, and Andreas Rauber. 2008. Rhyme and style features for musical genre classification by song lyrics. In *Ismir*, pages 337–342.

Ryan McDonald, Keith Hall, and Gideon Mann. 2010. Distributed training strategies for the structured perceptron. In *Human Language Technologies: The 2010 Annual Conference of the North American Chapter of the Association for Computational Linguistics*, pages 456–464. Association for Computational Linguistics.

Tomas Mikolov, Kai Chen, Greg Corrado, and Jeffrey Dean. 2013. Efficient estimation of word representations in vector space. *arXiv preprint arXiv:1301.3781*.

Frank Rosenblatt. 1958. The perceptron: a probabilistic model for information storage and organization in the brain. *Psychological review*, 65(6):386.

David E. Rumelhart, Geoffrey E. Hinton, and Ronald J. Williams. 1985. Learning internal representations by error propagation. Technical report, Institute for Cognitive Science, University of California.

Stacy L. Smith, Marc Choueiti, Katherine Pieper, Hannah Clark, Ariana Case, and Sylvia Villanueva. 2019. Inclusion in the recording studio? Gender and race/ethnicity of artists, songwriters & producers across 700 popular songs from 2012-2018. USC Annenberg Inclusion Initiative.

Nitish Srivastava, Geoffrey Hinton, Alex Krizhevsky, Ilya Sutskever, and Ruslan Salakhutdinov. 2014. Dropout: a simple way to prevent neural networks from overfitting. *The journal of machine learning research*, 15(1):1929–1958.

Alper Kursat Uysal and Serkan Gunal. 2014. The impact of preprocessing on text classification. *Information Processing & Management*, 50(1):104–112.

**Association for Computational Linguistics**
209 N. Eighth Street
Stroudsburg, Pennsylvania 18360

ISBN 978-1-5108-9443-3

9 781510 894433

CURRAN ASSOCIATES INC.
proceedings.com